Inside Banking

A Financial Guide for Canadians

Facts and tips about the Canadian financial system
for residents and new immigrants

Inside Banking ©2015 Artem Bytchkov
Additional print and eBook copies can be purchased through Amazon.
Library and Archives Canada Cataloguing in Publication
Bytchkov, Artem, 1978–, author
Inside Banking / Mr. Artem Bytchkov, PFP, FMA

ISBN-13: 978-150-8490289
ISBN-10: 150 849 0287

SOLA
ROSA
This book was produced by Sola Rosa Publishing, Canada.
Our mission is to publish only books that help people feel good or help them live better.
You can contact the author at contact@artemfinancial.ca

Printed in the U.S.
Book edited by Christa Bedwin.
Cover design: Sean Young.
Book layout: Raaj Chandran.

Inside Banking

A Financial Guide for Canadians

Facts and tips about the Canadian financial system
for residents and new immigrants

Mr. Artem Bytchkov, PFP, FMA

CONTENTS

INTRODUCTION

I have worked in the Canadian banking system for many years, and I have noticed that most Canadians are not aware of all the options available to them.

This book contains useful information for people born in Canada, those who have lived in this country for quite a while, and people who have arrived in Canada recently.

Once you read it, you will know more about the banking system than most other Canadians do.

This book does not generally promote specific programs, investments, or banks. When I do recommend something in particular, this is based on unbiased advice, and I still lay out all of your options in detail.

While you can find most of the information in this book free of charge, in particular on the internet, the problem is that you need to know what to search for to begin with (and as I mention above, many people are not aware of all the options).

Likewise, simply asking at your bank may not result in you learning all of the options presented here.

This book summarizes the information that it is good for you to know, to help you talk to your banker. It summarizes financial subjects in simple language and illustrates them with examples.

I have found that most people know much more about investing than banking. For example, they might know the difference between an ETF and a mutual fund, but not know the difference between a certified cheque and a bank draft.

I am absolutely convinced that even if you are a financially savvy person, you will still learn something new in this book.

This book consists of two major parts:

- Assets (what you own)
- Liabilities (what you owe, i.e. your debts)

If your assets exceed your liabilities, your net worth is positive. If your liabilities are more than your assets, your net worth will be negative.

Other issues covered in this book include insurance, power of attorney, credit history, cash flow, and more. Those issues are not related to your net worth directly, but it is impossible to achieve a positive net worth without proper protection, positive cash flow, etc. (let alone lottery and inheritance).

Do not take this book as personal financial or legal advice since the information provided here is general and might differ (somewhat) from information you would get from your financial advisor or a banker.

I provide no guarantees for the guidance and information given herein.

While this information can guide you to make good decisions, it is not intended as a substitute for professional advice.

Please visit www.insidebanking.ca.

Artem Bytchkov, PFP, FMA

PFP: Personal Financial Planner

FMA: Financial Management Advisor

Part 1: Assets

Assets can only be of two types:

- assets that appreciate in value (art, collectibles, precious metals, diamonds, etc.)

- assets that generate income (real estate, GICs, bonds, etc.)

Some assets may appreciate (or depreciate) in value and generate income (e.g. real estate).

Some investments can be used either for asset appreciation or income generation, depending on how you use them.

For example, if you buy some farmland you can either grow food there and the land will probably appreciate in value as a result, or you can rent out the land and it will generate income.

When you buy an asset, you should know in advance the reason you buy it: either for income generation or for appreciation in value.

If you buy an asset for a wrong reason, you can lose a lot of money.

For example, if you make a real estate investment, which should be considered an income asset, but you merely expect it to go up in value instead, you may be disappointed with your return.

Usually there is no crucial difference in the service that big banks, small community banks, and credit unions provide. Hereafter, they are all called "banks."

However, there is a big difference between banks and credit unions in guarantees that you get when depositing money there.

All banks are covered by CDIC insurance (explained below) for up to a certain limit, but all credit union accounts are guaranteed for an unlimited amount by Provincial Credit Union Deposit Guarantee Corporations.

Hereafter, when I use the term "financial institution" (FI), it refers to any financial company that lends or collects money after providing a service and may check credit history (e.g. a finance company, a broker, a cell phone company, a car dealer, etc.).

TIP 1
Tangible assets

Tangible assets (e.g. collectibles, precious metals, diamonds, real estate) incur expenses such as storage fees, insurance, alarm system, etc. Non-tangible assets, also known as "paper assets," do not usually incur (or have very few) expenses.

Chapter 1: TYPES OF INVESTMENTS — REGISTERED AND NON-REGISTERED

There are two types of investments in Canada: registered and non-registered.

Registered vs. Non-registered Investments

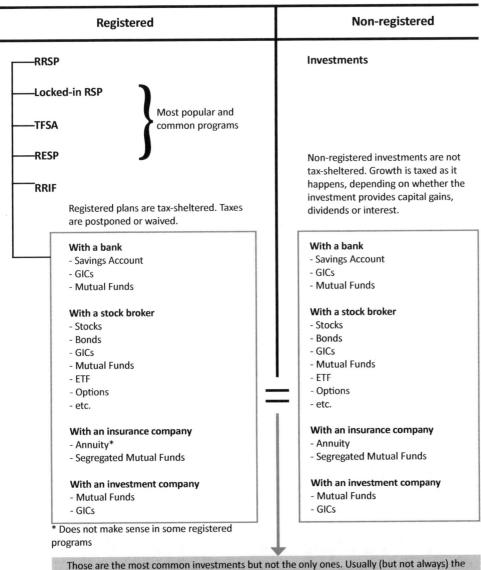

* Does not make sense in some registered programs

Those are the most common investments but not the only ones. Usually (but not always) the same investments can be held in non-registered and registered accounts.

As you can see from the table, investments held in non-registered accounts and registered programs are usually the same. However, some restrictions apply to registered programs. If you want to know more about qualified investments for registered programs, please follow this link:

http://artemfinancial.ca/links/qualified-investments

Some other investments that can be held in registered retirement savings plans (RRSPs) are listed here. These items tend to be less well known, and so less used, but can still be good options.

- **Debentures**: bonds that are not backed by collateral

- **Equity-linked notes**: bonds where the final payout is based on the return of the underlying equity or equities

- **Market-linked GICs**: guaranteed investment certificates (GICs) where the return depends on the underlying stock market

- **Mortgages secured by real estate property**: the so-called "RRSP mortgages." You can invest in private mortgages backed by Canadian real estate. With a self-directed mortgage your RRSP becomes the mortgage holder. You set up a mortgage just like you would at any financial institution, but instead of making payments to your financial institution, payments are made to your RRSP and you also keep the interest. Not many companies (called "trustees") deal with RRSP mortgages. They have to be approved under the National Housing Act. Some of the trustees are: Olympia Trust, Canadian Western Trust, and B2B Trust.

- **Rights and warrants**: give shareholders the right to buy more shares at a certain price by a certain date

- **Covered calls, long calls, and LEAPS (long-term equity anticipation securities).** These contracts give the buyer the right (but not the obligation) to buy or sell an underlying asset, usually stocks. The seller of the option has to fulfill the transaction if the buyer decides to use (exercise) his or her option prior to its expiration.

- **Gold and silver certificates**: physical certificates, similar to paper banknotes, that entitle the holder to the specified value of gold or silver

Note: I recommend the report "How to Invest in, Buy, Sell, Store, and Insure Precious Metals in Canada." Please visit http://artemfinancial.ca/links/metals to read it.

Non-registered accounts

A non-registered account is a non-tax-sheltered account where you can hold different investments. "Non-tax-sheltered" means that you have to pay tax on any income, dividends, or capital gains that you earn. You are free to deposit and withdraw funds at any time.

Registered programs

Registered programs are tax-sheltered. This means that when you open a registered program, the Canada Revenue Agency (CRA) understands it as "please tax me a certain way" (it might postpone the tax or waive it, as with TFSAs). Some examples of registered programs are:

- RRSP (registered retirement savings plan) and Spousal RRSP

- TFSA (tax-free savings account)

- RESP (registered education savings plan)

- Locked-In RSP (called LRSP or LIRA)

- RRIF (registered retirement income fund)

- LIF (life income fund)

- RDSP (registered disability savings plan)

Each program corresponds to at least one separate account.

Note: Many people think that since Tax Free Savings Account (TFSA) has the words "savings account" in it, the money has to be deposited into a savings account.

However, this is not the case. A TFSA is a type of registered program, not an account. Accordingly, all the options listed for other investments also apply to TFSAs.

Each time you open one of those programs you must provide your social insurance number, because the Canada Revenue Agency wants to know what you opened and where. The reason is that CRA restricts how much money you can contribute in total to the same program (or, for example, in the case of LIRAs, how much your employer can contribute).

Additional restrictions apply to different registered programs. Note that you can open the same program in different financial institutions (CRA does not restrict that) with exception of an RDSP (registered disability savings plan). Most registered programs are personal rather than joint (however, some financial institutions allow RESPs to be owned jointly).

The difference between a program and an account is that a program may potentially correspond to several accounts. For example, when you open a non-registered GIC, it is just one GIC. However, when you open an RRSP (or any other registered program) it can correspond to various accounts such as savings accounts, GICs, and mutual funds.

The investment options listed in the table are the most common ones, but other investment options exist.

Why would you open a registered program with a bank if you can have almost the same options (and even more options) with a stock broker?

Here are a few reasons to consider:

1. Usually you have to pay an annual or quarterly fee to hold a registered program with a broker, but you usually pay nothing to hold a registered program with a bank.

2. There are two types of brokers: full-service brokers who provide investment advice for a substantial fee, and discount brokers who do not usually provide advice (hence no fee involved). The problem is that it only makes sense to deal with a full-service broker if you are investing a lot, because very few people are knowledgeable enough to manage or invest their money on their own.

3. Many discount brokers do not have offices, and you usually cannot meet an advisor face to face.

4. Many people prefer to keep money in a savings account or GIC, not in mutual funds, bonds or stocks.

5. You might not get all of the government grants (see below) if you open an RESP with a broker.

6. If you open a registered program with a bank, they will advise you about their own affiliated products, such as GICs and mutual funds.

If you open a registered program or non-registered account with a broker, you could buy most GICs and mutual funds available in Canada issued or managed by various financial institutions.

Typical investments and investment providers

Places where you keep a Registered Program or Non-Registered Account*			
Bank	Stock Broker	Insurance Company	Investment Company
You can invest in			
- Savings account (the same as savings deposit) - GICs affiliated with this bank - Mutual funds affiliated with this bank	- GICs - Stocks - Bonds - Mutual funds - ETFs and ETNs - Options - Other (less popular) investments such as gold or silver certificates or physical gold or silver**	- Segregated funds - Mutual funds - RRIF or LIF: you can buy annuities (annuities are discussed in the RRIF section). You can also buy deferred annuities with your RRSP but it is very uncommon. Since annuities are a stream of fixed payments, there is no point to having them in a program where you have to contribute yourself.	- GICs - Mutual funds usually affiliated with this investment company

*Note that you have more investment options for non-registered accounts.
Please visit http://artemfinancial.ca/links/qualified-investments.
**In addition to certificates you can also hold physical gold and silver. However, even if you hold bullion in your registered program, you cannot actually take physical possession of the product (it has to stay with your broker). Instead, you can only get the equivalent of the price of the commodity. All registered investments must be paper-based.

Chapter 1 notes

Please use this space for your notes.

Chapter 2: BANK ACCOUNTS

Regular (non-registered) bank accounts can be individual or joint. If a bank account (see types of bank accounts below) is a joint one, it can be either JOINT AND or JOINT OR.

- JOINT OR means that each of the owners can deposit and withdraw money.

- JOINT AND means that all of the owners of the account must be present to withdraw money from the account, but each of the owners can deposit money.

Debit cards of JOINT AND account owners will not allow them to withdraw money from ATMs (automated teller machines). Moreover, if the account is JOINT AND, all of the owners must be present to make changes (e.g. to change the account to JOINT OR, or to close the account).

If the account is JOINT OR, any one of the owners can close the account without permission from the other owner(s).

If you are the only owner of the account, you can add other owners. If your account is joint (JOINT OR or JOINT AND), all of the owners must be present to add additional owner(s). Owners cannot be removed from the account (except when the person passes away).

There are several types of bank accounts:
- chequing account and seniors' chequing account
- savings account
- student account
- youth account
- estate account
- USD chequing account
- USD savings account

TIP 2
For new immigrants

Choose an unlimited transaction account for a certain monthly fee. Such accounts might include other options such as free cheques or discounts for certain premium credit cards.

If you have just recently arrived in Canada, you may qualify for discounts or a fee waiver on the chequing account, so check this with your bank. Some banks provide one free chequing account for a certain period of time as a promo for new clients.

TIP 3
Accounts for new immigrants

To open an account, you have to have two pieces of government-issued identification, at least one of which has to be a photo ID (i.e. an ID with your photo on it). Note that certain IDs are not accepted by banks, e.g. the Firearms License or the Ontario Health Card (even if they bear your photo).

The most common photo acceptable pieces of identification are:

• driver's license
• passport (Canadian or foreign)
• citizenship card
• provincial identification card

The most common non-photo IDs are:

• social insurance number
• health card (certain provinces issue non-photo health cards)
• credit cards (with your name on it)
• Canadian birth certificate
• Canadian immigrant visa

If you are a new immigrant or if you are a foreign worker (with a valid work permit), you can provide your foreign passport and your immigrant visa or work permit.

If you have no photo ID, but you can provide two non-photo IDs, your account can still be opened but it will be "deposit only" until you provide a photo ID. "Deposit only" means that you will not be able to withdraw money from the account.

If you wish to obtain a Canadian photo ID, you can get a driver's license or a provincial identification card. Get further information from registry offices of the province you reside in.

Some banks offer accounts in currencies other than CAD (Canadian dollars) and USD (U.S. dollars).

Most of these accounts can be switched from one type to another (like changing chequing to savings) without changing the account number (which is very convenient if you have a direct deposit or withdrawal, either into or from this account).

Some accounts (such as chequing, some savings, student or even USD accounts) can have the overdraft protection option (explained below).

When you open a bank account, you usually get a debit card that you can use with ATMs and to pay in stores for your purchases.

You can think of a debit card as your immediate access to your bank accounts: each card has a number of so-called slots that are each associated with one of your chequing or savings accounts.

When you use your card you can choose (via the ATM or Interac payment screen) which slot (i.e. account) the money will be withdrawn from.

Your debit card has one primary chequing slot, one primary savings slot and a number of other (secondary chequing or savings) slots.

How do your debit card slots get linked to your actual bank accounts? When you open a bank account (either chequing or savings) you can ask the banker to attach this account to be the primary chequing or primary savings slot of your debit card.

If the primary chequing and savings slots are already used by your other accounts, the newly created account may be added to your other (secondary) chequing or savings slots (see Figure 1 below). Note that usually only CAD accounts can be attached to the primary slots of your debit card.

As mentioned above, when you use your debit card in stores you have to choose which account the money (for the payment) will be withdrawn from: primary chequing or primary savings. These are the only two options available when you pay in stores.

When you use your debit card with an ATM that belongs to your bank, you have more options:

- you can select from your primary chequing, primary savings or other (secondary) chequing or savings accounts

- you can withdraw money from any of these accounts

- you can deposit money to a particular account

When you use an ATM that belongs to a different bank, you can only choose to withdraw money from either your primary chequing or primary savings account.

Note that a chequing account does not have to be attached to a chequing slot of your debit card, although this is normally the case, by default. Thus, if you have two chequing accounts, one of them is usually attached to the primary chequing slot of your debit card, but the other chequing account may be attached to the primary savings slot or to the other (secondary) chequing slot.

The same is true of savings accounts: they do not have to be always attached to savings slots of your debit card, although this is normally the case, by default.

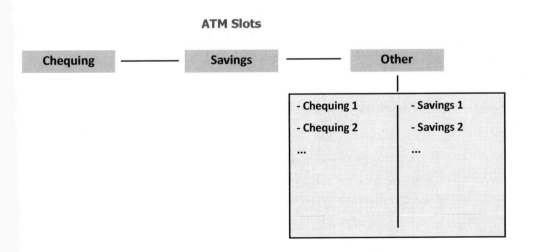

ATM Slots

| Chequing | — | Savings | — | Other |

- Chequing 1   - Savings 1
- Chequing 2   - Savings 2
...   ...

It is useful to keep in mind that if you withdraw money from ATMs belonging to banks other than your own, you will have to pay a fee to your bank (usually $1.50) and to the bank the ATM belongs to (usually $1.50 too). If you have an account with premium services it might cover the withdrawal fee of YOUR bank, but you will still have to pay the other bank fee.

When you use your debit card abroad, you only have access to your primary chequing account (applicable to both store purchases and ATM withdrawals). Since usually only a CAD account can be attached to a primary slot of your debit card, it means that you can only have access to one of your CAD accounts abroad.

When you pay for your purchase or withdraw money from an ATM, the money will be exchanged to the local currency. Note that even if you are visiting the United States and you have a USD account opened in Canada, you will not be able to use it. You will still only have access to your CAD accounts, and the money will be exchanged for you from CAD to USD.

A chequing account is for day-to-day transactions. It normally has a monthly fee (which some banks can waive if you meet particular criteria, such as keeping a certain balance on your account).

Monthly cycles (for the purpose of monthly statements, the limit of transactions, etc.) do not always have to start on the first of each month. It depends on the specific bank you deal with.

Your monthly fee is the same each month, regardless of the number of days in a particular month.

Chequing accounts may have limited or unlimited transactions. If you choose an account with limited transactions, each additional transaction over the limit will cost you money per withdrawal. (A withdrawal is when money is taken out (withdrawn) from the account. This includes when you withdraw with a teller or from the

TIP 4
4-digit PIN numbers

When selecting a PIN number for your debit card, use 4 digits.

Most ATMs in Canada will accept PINs with up to 6 digits, but some machines (in Canada and worldwide) only accept 4 digits.

If you have more than 4 digits in your PIN and the ATM does not accept more than 4, you will not be able to use your debit card.

ATM, pay a bill, or purchase something in a store using your debit card.)

Here are some ways to minimize the number of withdrawals in a limited transactions account and save on fees per additional withdrawal:

- Use your credit card if you have one. All credit card transactions are free, and you should pay your credit card bill only once a month (i.e. only one transaction per month).

- Ask for a Visa debit card if your bank offers one (see explanation in the credit card section). With some banks, purchases made with your Visa debit do not count towards the monthly debit transaction limits of your chequing account.

- Take advantage of the cash back option: some stores will allow you to withdraw money along with your payment. After you enter your PIN number, the Interac payment machine may ask if you want to also withdraw cash (cash back). This will save you one transaction.

Deposits to chequing accounts are usually free of charge.

Chequing accounts

Chequing accounts can be in US or Canadian currencies. You do not usually earn any interest for keeping money in a chequing account.

Most banks will switch your chequing account to a seniors' chequing account when you (or the eldest account holder, in case the account is joint) turn 60. Once the chequing account turns into a seniors' chequing account, banks will stop charging you the monthly fee.

While some banks will allow unlimited transactions on seniors' accounts, others will only allow a certain number of transactions for

> **TIP 5**
> **Transfers are free**
>
> Transfers are usually free of charge, depending on your bank.
> You can transfer money from your savings account to the chequing account and vice versa, and it will not count as a transaction or withdrawal.

> **TIP 6**
> **Save banking fees**
>
> Unfortunately, most banks charge fees for chequing accounts.
> To save on banking fees, you can switch your accounts to savings accounts (which are free if you make no, or a limited number of, transactions) and open a new free "unlimited transactions" account with a virtual bank, a credit union, or a community bank.
> Most of your transactions will probably be online, through an ATM, or with your debit card anyway, so there is no point paying a monthly fee for a chequing account.
> If you need to make a transaction with a teller (e.g. money wire), you can go to your physical bank and they will take money from your savings account. Switching banks is not convenient, but think how much money you will save over time.
> If enough people listen to this advice, banking fees for chequing accounts will become either lower or will be altogether eliminated.

free. In many cases the switch happens automatically when you (or the eldest account holder) turn 60, but you will sometimes need to request it yourself.

The switch does not change your account number. The seniors' rebate does not apply to other (non-chequing) accounts.

Savings accounts

Savings accounts are – as the name implies – to save money. Money sitting in the savings account earns simple interest which is usually calculated daily but is deposited to your savings account monthly. Deposits to your savings account are usually free, but you are allowed only a limited number of free withdrawals monthly. If you exceed your free monthly withdrawals, you have to pay for each additional withdrawal.

Since the point of a savings account is to earn interest, ask your banker which account earns the highest interest on the balance (banks usually have different types of savings accounts, and the interest they pay differs from one savings account to another). Savings accounts may be in US or Canadian currency, but some banks might offer savings accounts in different currency.

Note: Virtual banks

Virtual banks (banks that exist online but do not have, or have very few, offices that you can visit) often offer free chequing accounts. Some of them even pay interest on your balance in a chequing account. Those chequing accounts are free regardless of your daily balance or the number of transactions you are going to make.

Virtual banks have fewer expenses and they can afford to offer these services for free, while most bricks and mortar banks charge monthly fees for chequing accounts (it is one of their major sources of revenue).

If you decide to open an account with a virtual bank, make sure that it is listed on the Canada Deposit Insurance Corporation website at http://artemfinancial. ca/links/cdic-members.

Virtual banks offer savings accounts, too. Interest you earn on a virtual savings account is usually higher (and sometimes much higher) than what you can get with a bricks and mortar bank or credit union.

Example: Savings account interest

You have $1,000 sitting in your savings account for one month and the annual interest on this account is 1.25%.

The interest calculation is as follows (assuming 365 days in a year and 31 days in a month).

$$\left(\left(\frac{\$1000 \times 1.25\%}{100\%}\right)/365 \text{ days}\right) \times 31 \text{ days} = \$1.06$$

As mentioned, savings accounts earn simple interest monthly. However, if the money sits in the account for over one month, the calculation on already earned interest becomes compound (you earn interest on already earned interest).

The interest calculation for the second month is as follows (assuming 365 days in a year and 30 days in a month).

$$\left(\left(\frac{\$1001.06 \times 1.25\%}{100\%}\right)/365 \text{ days}\right) \times 30 \text{ days} = \$1.028$$

The Rule of 72 for investment doubling

There is a method to calculate the approximate time required for your investment to double, called the Rule of 72.

Divide 72 by the interest rate per period to get the approximate number of periods required for investment doubling.

For example, if you divide 72 by 1.25% annually, you get 57.6, which means that it will take (approximately) 57.6 years for your money to double with the annual interest of 1.25%. You can use the same method to calculate what interest you need to receive to double your money in a known period of time.

Student account

A student account is a day-to-day chequing account.

Most student accounts are free (or have reduced fees compared to regular chequing accounts). You can have a student account as long as you are attending school. Usually banks do not care how old you are. As long as you are enrolled in school you can have this type of account.

Banks request your school's proof of enrolment every year in order for you to maintain this account. You do not need to be a full-time student. Even if you attend school part time you will qualify for a student account with most banks.

Sometimes student accounts offer discounts on student credit card fees.

Youth account

Most banks have accounts for children and youth (below 18 or 19 years of age). A youth account can be opened under the child's name or can be opened jointly with the child and his or her parent(s) and/or grandparent(s). In many cases, this type of account is a hybrid between a chequing and savings account, meaning that you and/or your child can use it for day-to-day transactions, and the money in the account still earns some interest. Youth accounts are usually free of charge, and your child can get a debit card to use the account and online banking.

US Dollar chequing or savings accounts in Canada

People usually keep these accounts if they go to the United States of America or have a US dollar credit card.

The purpose of keeping a US dollar account is to avoid exchange commissions when withdrawing US dollars. As with Canadian dollar accounts, you may have chequing or savings accounts in USD.

Most of the information covered for Canadian dollar accounts above also applies to US dollar accounts. For example, savings accounts pay some interest on the balance, and chequing accounts have a monthly fee (which might be waived if certain conditions are met) and allow a certain number of free transactions per month.

With most banks, you cannot access a USD account (opened in Canada) at an ATM abroad. You can only access your primary chequing account in CAD.

In other words, if you are in the U.S.A. and you want to withdraw USD, you will still have to pay a cross-border fee and an exchange fee. Ask your bank if you can withdraw US dollars from your USD account when you travel abroad.

Some banks let you open a USD account in the U.S.A., with an affiliated US bank. This might be a better idea than to have a USD account in Canada if you travel often to the U.S.A. and want to use this account.

Estate account

An executor or administrator or liquidator (the exact term depends on the province) of the estate of a deceased person may open an estate account for tasks such as managing the estate bills, paying taxes, and distributing money to beneficiaries. A deceased person's personal accounts are usually closed or frozen when the person dies.

Bank fees on estate accounts can often be waived if the executor requests it. The account can only be accessed by the executor or administrator or liquidator of the estate. There is no point in opening an estate account if the deceased person did not have any money or had only debts.

If you are the executor, you can ask the bank to pay the bills of the deceased person and the funeral expenses from the deceased person's account. Never throw away receipts you get because if you cannot explain and prove why you spent the money of the deceased, you will be liable.

Cheques

The two common types of cheques are personal cheques and bank cheques (bank drafts). Traveller's cheques are a third type of cheques that are rarely used except for when you travel and do not want to take cash with you. The use of traveller's cheques is in decline since there are better alternatives such as credit cards.

If you do not have any cheques and need just one or two, some banks have counter cheques which they can print for you, often for free.

This way you do not need to order cheque books, which are quite expensive. Note that not all banks offer counter cheques.

TIP 10
Free cheques

If you need to order a personal cheque book, you may want to consider switching your account to a premium one where free cheques are included as part of the service package.

With some premium chequing accounts, you can order an unlimited number of personal cheques, but it still takes time to order and receive them.

You can place a stop payment on a cheque that you wrote and the cheque will not be honoured. Stop payment requests cost money.

To place a stop payment, you must indicate:

- the exact amount

- the date of the cheque

- the name of the payee

- the account number on the cheque

- the cheque number

Do not use this option unless you absolutely have to, since your bank might save this incident in its records which might affect your credit history with the bank. If you write a cheque and there is not enough money in your bank account to cover it, you will be charged a not sufficient funds (NSF) fee of around $40–$50.

Certified cheques

If you give a cheque to someone and this person does not trust you or needs the money immediately, they can go to the branch (sometimes to the same branch where your account was opened) and the bank will verify that sufficient funds exist in the account to honour the cheque.

A certified cheque cannot "bounce," since those funds are set aside in the bank's internal account. Banks charge for the service of certifying the cheque (the fee might be lower if you are a client of that bank or the fee may be waived if you have a premium service fee account with that bank).

> **TIP 11**
> **Should you include your address on your cheques**
>
> It is a good idea NOT to include your address and telephone number on your cheques, for two reasons.
>
> First, it is possible that you will move or change your telephone number.
>
> The second reason is related to privacy: the fewer people who know or can see your personal information, the better your privacy is protected.
>
> Keep in mind that identity theft is not uncommon. People whose identity is stolen usually spend hundreds of hours trying to clear their credit history and prove that they did not spend the money they are liable for.
>
> In any event, note that people who accept your cheques typically trust you, and they do not care where you live and what your telephone number is.

TIP 12
Pre-authorized payments

If you pre-authorize any service providers (for example, a gym or an insurance company) to withdraw money from your account on a monthly or bi-weekly basis, you might not be able to stop withdrawals even after your contract with the company has expired.

You can do a stop payment order with your bank, but if the provider changes the amount of the payment the payment will go through.

If the company keeps charging you, the only guaranteed way to stop withdrawals is to close the account.

Companies are usually quite good with ceasing withdrawals after they stop providing services, but in case of miscommunication or disagreement, it might be very problematic to cancel such pre-authorized withdrawals.

Having said that, try to avoid releasing your banking information to service providers, and whenever possible provide them with your credit card details instead.

It is much easier to stop payments through a credit card: you simply need to call your credit card company to resolve the issue.

Here are several other reasons why you should ask service providers for monthly bills (to pay them yourself) or give them your credit card number for preauthorized payments.

Release on hold

When you deposit a non-certified personal cheque payable to you, it may be put on hold by your bank. Cheques are usually put on hold for four business days, but foreign cheques or cheques from small community banks or credit unions may be put on hold for a longer period of time.

Depending on your release amount, you may or may not get access to the funds in full or partially before the cheque is cleared. Your release amount depends on your relationship with your bank and/or your credit history.

The longer you stay with your bank and the more products you have with it, the larger your release amount may be. It can be increased upon your request, and the bank has the right to decrease it if you present financial risk to the bank. When you are a new client, the release amount is usually very small.

Regardless of whether you deposit a cheque at an ATM or with a teller, it will be on hold for the same period of time. However, you may be able to convince a teller to reduce this period or not to put your cheque on hold at all.

If you deposit cash with an ATM it will be still put on hold, because ATMs cannot detect exactly how much money you deposit. In this case, the release period depends on when the bank will process the envelope with the cash that you deposited.

The release amount is not applicable to Direct Deposit (e.g. when your wage is deposited to your account directly) since these funds are cleared right away, and the funds become available in full.

Information for new immigrants: Why and when do people use cheques?

You cannot pay for everything with just your debit or credit card. You are not allowed to pay off debt with borrowed money.

For example, you cannot pay a loan with your credit card. When you buy something very expensive, such as a car, you cannot use your credit card either.

If you need to pay rent, most landlords will not accept cash or a credit card, but will accept cheques.

Finally, some employers still pay their employees by physical pay cheques rather than deposit their wage directly to their accounts.

At the same time, there is a lot of fraud involved with cheques, and banks want to protect themselves by putting cheques on hold.

Another very common type of cheque is a void cheque (or as many people call it a "direct deposit form").

Companies who need to deposit money to your account or withdraw it from your account (such as insurance companies or utility companies) need to know your banking information, so they ask for a void cheque, which is a regular cheque (which has your banking information) that is crossed out and has the word "void" written on it. If you do not have any cheques, you can request a Direct Deposit form from your bank instead.

If you have questions about your rights and responsibilities when you open a bank account or cash a government cheque, please go to the Financial Consumer Agency of Canada site at www.fcac-acfc.gc.ca.

Every time the service provider takes money from your credit card, you earn cash back or reward points (if you have such rewards, and most cards now do).

If you have limited transactions on your account and you have pre-authorized withdrawals, you waste your transactions. Transactions with any credit card are unlimited.

If there is a pre-authorized payment from your credit card, you postpone the real payment until you pay your credit card bill.

To prevent scams, do not let anybody know your banking information.

Personal financial information should not be disclosed, especially account numbers and PINs (this applies to credit card numbers too, but they are much easier to replace in case of a fraud).

Bank drafts

Bank drafts are cheques issued by banks, and they have not been put on hold until recently. Most banks have recently started putting them on hold, because of a rising number of fraud incidents associated with them. In many cases, banks will not put a bank draft on hold if you can provide a receipt confirming that you purchased it from another bank.

Bank drafts will incur a fee. However, if you have a premium account the draft might be issued free of charge. Even if you do not have this type of account, you may still ask your bank to issue a draft for free. Asking never hurts, and it can save you money.

If for any reason you do not use the draft, you may bring it back and the bank will deposit the money back to your account – it never expires.

If the draft gets lost, you can go to your nearest branch and easily cancel it. It will not be easy for someone else to cash the draft.

Neither personal cheques nor bank drafts have any amount limit you can write on them (as long as you have enough money in your account).

You can order and write personal cheques from your US account, but the cheque will be good only in Canada. To deposit it in a bank in the U.S.A., you have to ask for a US money order.

If you receive a cheque from abroad, you may deposit it to your Canadian account and the currency will be exchanged to CAD (unless you deposit a US cheque to a US account).

Note: If you deposit a foreign cheque, you should mention that to the teller. Otherwise, it might be deposited as a Canadian cheque in CAD (by mistake) without exchange. Do not deposit foreign cheques in the automated teller machine.

Chapter 2 notes

Please use this space for your notes.

Chapter 3: INVESTMENTS

Investment income for non-registered accounts

Here are three types of income from investments, and how they are taxed:

- Interest is passive income from bonds, savings accounts, and GICs. It is taxed exactly as employment income.

- Dividend is what companies pay out to their owners (shareholders). Dividends received from Canadian public companies (i.e. shares of Canadian companies that are traded on Canadian Exchanges) are taxed less than your employment income (or interest) because of dividend tax credits. Foreign dividends do not qualify for tax credits and are taxed differently.

- Capital gain (or capital loss) is when your investment is sold with a profit (or loss). It is taxed at the lowest rate of these three types of income.

You must declare interest and dividends on your income tax return the year you receive them.

If you have a 5-year-term GIC and you will receive interest only in 5 years, you still have to declare interest income on your income tax return every year during these 5 years (not necessarily equal amounts, depending on the GIC type). Ask your bank to provide you with a T5 tax slip (Relevé 3 in Quebec) showing how much interest you have earned.

Declaration of capital gain or loss is deferred to the year you actually realize the gain or loss. You will not necessarily have to pay tax on this income as you might have personal tax credits or deductions, but you must still declare this income.

TIP 13
Moving your investments to a registered program

You can move your investments from a non-registered account to a registered program without selling them (assuming you have enough room in the registered program and other conditions are met). It makes sense to move interest- or dividend-bearing investments to a registered program, tax-wise.

However, please keep in mind: If your investment has a gain and you move it "in kind" (i.e. without selling it), you will generate capital gain and you will have to declare it the year of transfer.

If your investment has a loss and you move it in kind, you will NOT generate capital loss and you will not be able to declare capital loss for this investment at all, including in future years. As a result, it would be wise to sell this investment first and then buy the same investment in your registered program after 30 days. (The superficial loss rules state that you will have to wait 30 days before repurchasing the same investment again; otherwise, the loss will be omitted.)

Why invest?

Why would you want to invest at all in risky assets (mutual funds/stocks/bonds), instead of simply keeping the money in a savings account?

As they say, there are three certain things in life: inflation, taxes, and death.

The first reason to invest in risky assets is to protect the purchasing power of your money. Money that is not invested loses its purchasing value due to inflation (i.e. rising prices). Without going into details about why inflation exists in the first place, you have no choice but to accept it as a fact and to take measures to protect your wealth.

The second reason is to grow your wealth (and increase its purchasing power).

The biggest expense of your life is most likely not your mortgage or student loans but your taxes. You can think of inflation as an additional "hidden tax."

Your investment in a GIC or a savings account will not provide you with a rate of return higher than the rate of inflation, so you lose the purchasing power when investing in a GIC or savings account every single year. On top of that, if your investment is in a non-registered account, you have to pay taxes on earned interest annually, so you lose even more!

If you want to protect your purchasing power, you have to consider alternatives to GICs and savings accounts. You do not need to invest all your money. Cash is still a very valuable part of the portfolio.

However, it is not wise to invest only in GICs for decades.

TIP 14
Corporate class

Some investment companies offering mutual funds have a series of shares called Corporate Class. Its advantage is that you can switch between different funds within a given group of funds (or "class") without any capital gains or losses being realized.

So if, for example, you own Fund A in the class series and you want to switch to Fund B in the class series (both funds must be from the same investment company), you can switch between them without realizing capital gain (or loss).

The MER (Management Expense Ratio) of class funds is sometimes higher than the MER of the same non-class funds.

Guaranteed Investment Certificates

A guaranteed investment certificate (GIC) is a term deposit investment. When you buy a GIC from a financial institution, you are agreeing to lend them your money for a certain period of time (months or years).

GICs are one of the safest ways to invest: you are guaranteed to get the amount you deposited back at the end of the investment term along with the interest, if you hold the GIC till maturity. GICs are called "cash" because they do not fluctuate in value, and they are guaranteed.

If you hold a GIC in your non-registered account, you have to claim the interest (if it is known in advance) as income for tax purposes every year, regardless of when you are paid the interest (once a year or at maturity in 2–5 years). If you do not receive a tax slip (T5 or Relevé 3 in Quebec) from your bank, ask them how much interest you have earned. Banks do not usually send slips if the interest per account is less than $50. However, you are still responsible for claiming interest even if you have not received any tax slip from your financial institution.

To invest in a non-registered GIC with a bank, you will first have to open a separate non-registered GIC account just for GICs. You can buy more than one GIC in the same GIC account.

If you want to invest in a registered GIC, you do not typically need to open a separate account just for GICs. With most banks you can use the same registered investment account (such as RRSP or TFSA) where you hold your registered mutual funds and the registered savings deposit or account.

The most common types of GIC are:

*   redeemable GIC
*   non-redeemable GIC
*   market-linked GIC

In addition, a bank might have a unique type of GIC that no other bank has.

Redeemable GICs can and non-redeemable GICs cannot be redeemed (cashed out), as the names imply.

The crucial difference between redeemable and non-redeemable GICs is that you can break your redeemable GIC anytime without a problem, and you might get some interest for the period you held it (although you will probably not get any interest if you held it for less than 30 or 31 days, depending on your bank). Since they are "breakable," banks give you a lower interest on redeemable GICs than on non-redeemable ones, for the same term.

Non-redeemable GICs cannot be broken and money cannot be withdrawn. You will not be able to convince the bank's branch manager that you did not understand what you were signing when investing in a non-redeemable GIC.

In some circumstances (such as an accident or serious illness) banks may agree to break a non-redeemable GIC, but you should not count on it, and you will not get any interest in most cases.

Market-linked GICs offer the best of both worlds: the security of a GIC and the potential growth of the equity markets. These GICs are usually 3- or 5-year GICs whose return is linked to the performance of a specific stock index, such as the Canadian S&P or TSX 60 Index (i.e. the index of the largest 60 Canadian publicly traded companies) or one of the international indexes.

Your original investment is guaranteed if the underlying stock market index is lower at maturity than when you initially purchased the GIC (you get 100% of your investment back), but you profit if the underlying stock market index is higher at maturity.

The profit depends on the terms of the market-linked GIC and how much higher the underlying stock index is. The return of these types of GIC is not known in advance.

3. Typically, you have to hold a GIC (even if it is a redeemable one) for 30 days to get some interest, i.e. if you break it prior to 30 days, you do not get any interest. Money in a savings account is accessible any time, and you earn interest even if you keep it there for just 1 day.

The minimum amount you can invest in a GIC is typically $500. You do not pay any fees when you buy GICs. In general, the longer the term, the higher the interest rate you will earn. The interest on your GIC may be paid monthly, every 3 months, every 6 months, once a year or only at the maturity date. The bigger the amount, the higher the interest you would get.

Note: If you require the interest on a GIC to be paid earlier (i.e. more frequently than annually), then the interest rate will be lower.

To find out more about indexes, see below.

Market-linked GICs might qualify for the Canadian Deposit Insurance Corporation insurance in case of a bank failure. Please visit www.cdic.ca for more information.

Mutual funds

Most mutual funds consist of three components:

- stocks (also called shares or equities)
- bonds (also called fixed income)
- cash

Funds might have 0% on one of these components (e.g. cash 5%, bonds 0%, and stocks 95%), but all the components will be mentioned in the investment summary of a mutual fund.

Example: Mutual fund

Cash	$3,000
10 Shares company A	$1,000
20 Shares company B	$4,000
40 Bonds company C	$2,000
50 Bonds company D	$10,000
Total Value of the Fund	$20,000

10%

If you invest $2,000 in this fund, you become a 10% owner of the whole fund and you will own:

Cash	$300
10 Shares company A	$100
20 Shares company B	$400
40 Bonds company C	$200
50 Bonds company D	$1,000
Your investment value	$2,000

belongs to you

}

The fund manager merely manages investments for you. You and other investors are the owners of the investments in the mutual fund.

The asset size of mutual funds is of course much larger than $20,000, but the idea is the same regardless of the fund asset size.

Stocks

A stock, also known as a share or an equity, is a representation of the ownership of a company and its earnings.

Example:

You and your friend decide to start a business. You open a corporation with 40% shares owned by your friend and 60% shares owned by you.

As a company owner, you and your friend are entitled to your share of the company's profits, 60% and 40%, respectively. (To simplify, in this example I will refer to the corporation as a company.)

As the company owner you have several options:

- You can work in the company, hold its shares, and receive dividends (i.e. you are the owner AND an employee).

- You can hire someone to work for your company and not work yourself (i.e. you are just the owner but not an employee).

- You can sell all your shares and work in the company (i.e. you are no longer the owner of the company, but just an employee).

Note: If you sell your company, you might qualify for $800,000 Lifetime Capital Gains Exemption to reduce your tax. Please visit http://artemfinancial.ca/links/cap-gain-exemption for more information.

There are several reasons to take money out of the company:

- to pay wages to employees

- to pay income (dividends) to the owners (i.e. "shareholders") of the company

- to repay capital or expenses to the shareholder

- to take a loan (i.e. borrow money from the company)

However, the company does not need to distribute ALL of the profit. It can retain some of the profit in the company and use it as its management decides.

Bonds

A bond is a debt security issued for a period of time to raise funds by borrowing. The issuer has to pay the lender interest and/or repay the principal (i.e. the initial investment) at a later date, called maturity. (The holder of the bond is the lender of money, the issuer of the bond is the borrower.)

Returning to the same small business example with 40%/60% ownership, if you decide to expand the company and you need money, the two most common options are to either ask your bank to lend money to your company or ask private lenders to do so.

There are many reasons for not wanting to deal with a bank.

Example: When private lenders agree to lend money to your company, if you take $5,000 for 5 years with the condition that your company will pay 5% interest annually, your company issues a bond promising to respect the interest payment (and the principal of $5,000 is paid back after 5 years, i.e. at the maturity of the bond).

As long as the company stays in business, it has to pay interest as promised (although in very rare cases it can skip those payments). Usually, but not always, the longer the term of the bonds, the higher the interest rate.

For the company that issues bonds, they are liabilities (the company has to pay interest on them), while for the lender bonds are assets (the lender receives interest on them plus their money back at maturity of the bond).

Accordingly, if someone buys bonds in a company or of the provincial or federal government, the investor lends money to these entities, which have to pay interest.

A rule of thumb is that the higher the risk, the higher the rate of return for the lender or investor. For example, corporate bonds generally pay higher interest than provincial bonds (everything else being equal) because the risk of a company going broke is higher than that of the provincial government.

Similarly, provincial bonds generally pay higher interest than the federal government bonds (everything else being equal) for the same reason: the risk of default is higher on the provincial level than on the federal one.

When comparing bonds of the same issuer, the longer the term of the bond, the more interest the lender should receive (everything else being equal).

Occasionally, long-term bonds pay less interest than short-term bonds; that is called an inverted yield curve.

Cash

When I speak about cash that mutual funds hold, I mean two types of assets:

- cash as everybody understands it

- short-term government or large company bonds

Since mutual funds hold considerable sums of money, they cannot keep the money in cash only. Therefore, they lend it to the government for short periods of time and earn some interest on it. Since the likelihood of the Canadian government going bust is insignificant, these bonds represent an extremely low risk.

Mutual funds have to hold cash (cash and short-term government bonds) for the following reasons:

- The manager of the mutual fund buys and sells investments for the mutual fund.

- The owners of the mutual fund have the right to sell (redeem) their shares and receive cash.

In theory, most investors buy shares when they expect the economy to be good and growing. As a result, businesses make money and have more profit, or in other words, the shares become more valuable.

Following the same logic, most investors get rid of shares and switch to something more predictable when the economy is not doing well.

Shares are supposed to be a riskier investment because nobody knows how much profit companies will make, if any.

On the other hand, investors may decide to buy bonds when they expect the economy to do badly and they want more stability (they want to receive known interest payments), and they may decide to sell bonds when the economy becomes better. Bonds are supposed to be a less risky investment because you know in advance how much interest you will get and how much money you will get back at the maturity of the bond (assuming companies stay in business and do not default).

However, even though in theory, bonds are supposed to be less risky and stocks more risky, they are actually both relatively risky investments because in both cases you can lose money even if the company whose shares you buy does not go out of business. If investors do not like some company or some sector of the economy, the shares of this company may go down significantly. Nothing may be wrong with the company itself or with this specific sector of the economy, but just because they are out of favour the shares may collapse in value.

If interest rates start to go up, bonds will go down in value (the opposite is true, as well).

Example: Bonds and interest rates

Investor A lends $1,000 to a company for 5% because the prime rate is 5%.

However, if the prime is going up to 6%, why would someone buy a bond from Investor A for $1,000 if they can buy a similar bond that pays 6% for the same $1,000?

In this case, the price of Investor A's bonds will go down in value. This matters only if Investor A wants to sell the bonds prior to their maturity; if they want to keep them to maturity (and receive their money back), such price fluctuations exist only on paper.

Interest rates have an inverse relationship with bond prices.

In summary, when bonds go down, shares tend to go up, and vice versa.

No mutual fund is a guaranteed investment, and they are long-term investments (except a money market fund, which can be used for a short-term time horizon).

- A mutual fund that has more stocks is associated with more risk and a higher rate of return than a mutual fund that holds fewer stocks.

- A mutual fund that has more bonds is associated with less risk and smaller fluctuations in the fund price than a mutual fund that holds fewer bonds.

However, in both classes of assets some investments are riskier than others.

For example, as mentioned earlier, provincial government bonds are riskier than federal government bonds.

Usually, the higher the risk, the higher the rate of return.

Three common sites for analyzing Canadian mutual funds are:

- www.morningstar.ca
- www.globefund.com
- www.fundlibrary.com

Some types of mutual funds

Usually, the higher the risk, the higher the rate of return.

Here are some further details of the different kinds of funds.

- **Money Market Funds** focus on short-term securities. They are considered to be the least risky of all mutual funds. They are designed to provide regular (low but usually stable) income to investors.

- **Bond Funds** provide income to their owners with some potential of capital appreciation. These funds normally pay income on a monthly, quarterly or annual basis. The risk is considered to be low to moderate, because you know in advance how much money you lend, how much money you should expect to get back at maturity, and how much interest you should get for lending your money.

- **Balanced Funds** provide income and capital appreciation (e.g. growth) while providing the benefit of diversification between bonds and stocks. Balanced funds invest in bonds and stocks in approximately equal proportion. However, they might have more stocks than bonds in which case the fund will deliver more capital appreciation and less income (similar to balanced growth funds). They might pay some income occasionally or on a regular basis.

- **Equity Funds** provide long-term capital appreciation and may pay dividend income. Usually, equity funds invest in stocks that are featured in the name of the fund (e.g. Asia Equity Fund invests mainly in Asia), but they may hold some bonds, too.

- **Fund of Funds** is an investment strategy of holding a portfolio of other investment funds rather than investing directly in shares, bonds, and/or other securities. A fund of funds allows investors to achieve a broad diversification and an appropriate asset allocation with investments in a variety of fund categories.

- **Index Funds** are mutual funds that comprise securities from a particular segment of the market (stock market, bond market, etc.). An index mutual fund is supposed to provide broad market exposure, low operating expenses (low Management Expense Ratio (MER, see explanation below) compared to other types of mutual funds), and low portfolio turnover (buying and selling of securities) rates because it is not actively managed. For an example of an index fund, consider funds tied to the S&P/TSX 60 index, one of the Canadian indexes representing the 60 biggest Canadian companies traded on the Toronto Stock Exchange. An index fund can represent a broad market (e.g. the stock market or bond market) or a specific sector of the market (e.g. energy stocks or municipal bonds).

What fund should you choose to invest in?

There is no perfect mutual fund. They are all risky.

For example, the Money Market rate of return is typically less than the rate of inflation so although you do not risk losing your principal, you still lose your purchasing power. This is obviously different from losing your principal, but losing purchasing power still counts as a risk.

The higher the risk of a mutual fund and the higher its volatility (these funds go up and down in value), the longer you should be holding it in your portfolio.

The best option for most people who want to invest in mutual funds is to invest on a weekly/bi-weekly/monthly basis rather than monitoring each fund's price fluctuation every trading day.

Note: If you are planning to invest in mutual funds, do not listen to the radio or newspapers that may claim the economy is or is not doing well, or may recommend that you should or should not invest now. The economy is NOT a stock market and stocks can go up in value when the economy is not doing well, and they can go down when the economy is doing well. There is, of course, still a correlation between the two. Independently of what you read in newspapers or hear in the news, stock market participants already know and take economic factors into account.

As you begin to properly understand the investments you hold or want to invest in, you become willing to accept more risk and more fluctuation in prices.

The cost of mutual funds

All funds have a management expense ratio (MER) that determines how much the mutual fund management company charges its clients for managing their money. Note that the MER is charged by all mutual funds, regardless of their performance (the MER includes almost all fees associated with owning a fund and is expressed as a percentage of the total assets in the fund).

A performance fee may sometimes be charged on top of the MER, and clients should normally expect better returns from such mutual funds because managers of these funds are interested to excel to get this performance fee. This fee is only charged if the fund exceeds a particular benchmark.

The daily prices of mutual funds that you see on different financial sites (e.g. sites mentioned earlier) are net, without the MER fee. For example, if you see that today the price of a mutual fund is $9 CAD, the MER fee has already been deducted. The price is the same whether you sell or buy this mutual fund.

TIP 16
Trust yourself first

Keep in mind that you are the person who knows best how to invest your money.

If or when you get recommendations from your financial advisor or banker, take them as merely recommendations and not instructions about what/when/how much to buy. Nobody cares about your money more than you do.

If something does not make sense to you, do not do it. When people listen to a professional advisor explaining investments to them (including situations when they do not quite understand what the advisor is talking about), they tend to think that the advisor really knows what to do with their money.

In my practice I have seen advisors who tell their clients how to invest their money, but who do not know what to do with their own money and ask advice from other advisors themselves.

When you buy a mutual fund, you might have some transaction costs.

There are two types of funds: load funds that have a sales charge, and no-load funds that do not have a sales charge.

The goal of a load fund is to keep the money invested for a longer period of time (and hence to collect the MER fee for a longer period of time). On the other hand, no-load funds allow more flexibility as they do not charge any type of transaction fee regardless of whether you buy or sell them.

There are normally three types of load funds in Canada: front-end, back-end, and low load funds.

- **The front-end load** is also known as the sales charge, which is a fee paid when you buy shares of that fund. This fee usually goes to the broker or salesperson that sells you the fund.

- **The back-end load** is also known as the deferred sales charge, which is a fee paid when you sell shares of that fund. This fee if paid goes to the mutual fund company (the broker or salesperson who sold you the fund receives their commission when the sale of the mutual fund takes place). If you hold the fund long enough (usually 5–7 years) you will not pay this fee when you sell the fund.

- **Low load** is very similar to deferred sales charge, but the period you have to hold the fund to avoid this fee is typically 3 years.

If a company sells a load fund, it usually also sells a similar fund as a no-load fund.

The MER fee on a no-load fund is higher than on a corresponding load fund, because the investor does not commit to stay with the company for any substantial period of time.

To distinguish between load and no-load funds, companies use series (which are marked by capital letters).

Example: No-Load vs. Front-End Load Balanced Mutual Funds

If company ABC manages a no-load balanced mutual fund and a front-end load balanced mutual fund, then the no-load fund could have the name of "ABC Balanced Fund Series A" and the front-end fund could have the name of "ABC Balanced Fund Series B."

| | No-Load Mutual Funds | Load Mutual Funds | |
		Front-End MFs	Back-End MFs
Fees	No fees when you buy or sell	Fees only when you buy	Fees when you sell within a certain period of time
MER	Higher than in similar load MFs	Lower than in similar no-load MFs	Lower than in similar no-load MFs

Theoretically, load funds should perform better than no-load funds (due to the lower MER fee), but this is not always the case. According to a survey by the mutual fund data analyzer Morningstar, no-load funds actually have a superior record to load funds over a long period of time.

Funds that impose no cost to purchase have outperformed those that brokers pay themselves to find for their clients.

Note: Most professionals think that asset allocation is the key to success in investing. In theory, when you put different investments together, one investment will go up, the other will go down, and you will make (or will not lose) money.

I tend to disagree. In my humble opinion, market timing is the most important strategy. Investment is a probability game so if the odds are in your favour, you will probably gain money. You might not invest in anything for years and keep money in a simple savings account, but if you wait till the stock market crashes (which is inevitable at some point), you can buy almost any shares or almost any equity mutual fund, and the probability is very high that you will make money in those investments.

It is very difficult to wait and do nothing for years when you watch the stock market moving higher up, but eventually it will fall 20–30%.

The absolute majority of people buy when stocks are high up and not when they are down.

You have to be scared (like everybody else) when you invest in stocks that have just fallen 20–30% or even 50%, but this way it is almost guaranteed that you will make money in the long run.

It might not be easy to invest when the stock market goes down because you need to check the status of the market on a regular basis. However, there is a relatively simple strategy that you can implement. It does not guarantee that you will make money, but at least you will have a "probability in your favour" strategy.

Please discuss this strategy with a qualified investment advisor and see if this strategy is suitable for you, as it is just a strategy and not a recommendation. It should be used only as a long-term strategy (10 years or more).

Before I discuss the technique, I have to talk about stock and bond markets in general.

Note: As mentioned above, when interest rates rise, bond values decrease. Interest rate cycles are very long; an average cycle is about 30 years long. Since today's interest rates are exceptionally low, they can only go up in the future, which means that the bond market will probably be going down for many years to come. If you invest for a long period of time in a Bond Mutual Fund or a Bond ETF, you will probably lose money. This logic leaves us with a simple conclusion: invest in stocks.

How to invest in stocks

Step 1. Decide how much you want to invest on a regular basis. There is no minimum or maximum, and it is up to you how much you want to invest.

Invest 50% of this amount on a regular basis in an index broad equity mutual fund (e.g. S&P 500 index mutual fund that represents the biggest 500 US companies), and put the remaining 50% into a simple savings account (choose a savings account with the highest interest rate).

The best way to invest is when money is taken from your account automatically without your involvement and is invested as mentioned above.

Step 2. When you hear everybody around you saying how bad the stock market is because it goes down and that the world is coming to an end – it is in fact quite probable that the stock market will start recovering soon: nothing goes up or down forever.

Check if your index fund is at least 20% down from its peak. If it is, take the money from your savings account (which you saved as explained above) and invest it into the same index mutual fund you have been investing in all along.

It is, however, much more difficult to put your finger on when the market is going to fall – even if everybody says how well their investments are performing, it does not necessarily mean the market is going to fall soon.

The reason is simple: people like to brag even about 5% they gained, but they usually do not speak about their losses until they have lost a lot of money. Then people cannot withstand any more losses, so they sell their losing investments and tell everybody how bad the stock market is. Markets usually go up slowly for a long period of time, but they fall fast and sharply.

Cash is a very valuable investment (if we do not have a very high inflation), so do not disregard it. Advisors often tell you that your money has to be invested 100% all the time. What they do not tell you is that they are paid more when you are fully invested. They are usually paid nothing when you wait and keep money in your savings account.

Step 3. It is impossible to predict when and how much the stock market will go up and down, which is why you should invest 50% on a regular basis and not wait until the market falls to invest everything.

Many studies show that very few people (including fund managers) can consistently outperform stock market returns. As a result, this strategy gives a better chance to make money than trying to choose the "right" fund and the "right" time.

Guidelines for buying mutual funds

1. Try to avoid funds with a high number of holdings in them (see Total Number of Holdings in the overview of the fund). Who is able to manage 500 different holdings? If it holds 1,000+ investments – the fund itself becomes THE MARKET, and it will not make a lot of money in the long run.

2. Try to avoid funds with a high turnover. A turnover with 100%+ means that all of the investments and more were bought or sold in the fund during a 12-month period. It costs you money when the fund manager buys and sells. The best investments are investments that are held for longer periods of time, not just several months.

3. Try to avoid exchange-traded notes, ETNs. They are not the same thing as exchange-traded funds, ETFs (see ETF vs. ETN in the glossary).

4. Try to avoid funds that have recently received favourable publicity. The reason is that many investors will flush the fund with their money, and the manager might not be able to put all this new money to good use.

5. You are not very likely to see good fund managers on TV since they are busy doing their jobs, plus they are usually well aware of the tendency mentioned above. They are not interested in getting too much new money, as they know they may underperform in the next few quarters and consequently lose that money due to redemption of unsatisfied clients.

6. The best of the best funds usually charge a performance fee on top of the MER, as they want to be paid extra for their extra performance. Those funds are usually equity funds, and they are riskier than the majority of equity funds. As a result, you should hold this kind of fund for many years and not compare its performance quarter to quarter. Do not avoid funds with performance fees, but also do not invest all your money there.

7. If you want to invest with a small investment management company, send them an email with a question to see how they reply. It is usually not important what they reply but if they reply at all. If the company does not reply to you then it does not matter how good their track record is. They do not care about their investors and you should avoid them.

8. This is one of the simplest but most powerful techniques to avoid bad investment companies. If they do not reply when you ask questions, they will also not reply when problems arise.

9. Try to avoid funds that claim to be the cheapest, biggest, newest, etc., since what you really want is to invest in the best ones, but no fund will ever claim precisely that.

10. Try to find out if the manager of the fund invests his or her own money in the fund they manage. It indicates that the manager believes in what they manage. Unfortunately, providing this information is not mandatory, and it is difficult to get. However, managers who invest their own money in the funds they manage are normally proud of that and will not hide it.

11. Comparing funds with a similar investment strategy across different investment companies (e.g. Bond A Fund vs. Bond B Fund), funds with a lower MER usually perform better.

12. Comparing funds with a similar investment strategy across different investment companies, smaller funds (in terms of its holdings) usually perform better than larger ones. It is easier to operate $200 million than $5 billion.

13. Comparing an index fund with a managed non-index fund that has a similar investment strategy (e.g. Bond Index A Fund vs. Bond B Fund), an index fund will usually perform better because of lower operating expenses and a low(er) portfolio turnover.

14. Comparing funds with a similar investment strategy, funds established in the last 12 months will usually perform better than older funds due to the following reasons. Newer funds do not have investments that could have generated losses, so they do not need to sell at loss. Newer funds are likely to be smaller and hence easier to manage. Finally, the manager of a newer fund has to work harder to prove themselves and is therefore more likely to provide better results.

15. Sector funds (e.g. Technology Fund, Resource Fund) provide extraordinary returns for only a certain period of time (they are cyclical). Once this sector is out of investors' favour, it is probably wise to stay away from it for a long period of time.

16. If you find a fund you want to invest in for a long period of time, find out if this fund has different series and review them. Find out which of the series has the smallest MER and why, and switch to it if that is appropriate (if you stay long term, they usually reduce series MER, but if you sell in a relatively short period of time after you bought it, they will charge you a redemption fee).

17. Examine commissions when you buy mutual funds. If you are not planning to stay with the mutual fund for a long period of time, avoid load funds and choose no-load ones instead.

18. Try to choose funds with a lot of cash. As explained earlier, cash is an excellent tool that allows funds to buy investments on sale when everybody else sells. (Probably the best site to review these recommendations is Morningstar at www.morningstar.ca.)

Note: In my opinion, the primary goal of most mutual fund companies is to avoid losing your money; they are less interested in growing it. I came to this conclusion based on my review of hundreds of mutual funds and the number of holdings they have.

In my opinion, it is virtually impossible for any mutual fund to beat its benchmark (e.g. S&P 500 as explained above) if it holds 200+ investments (and many of the mutual funds in Canada hold even more than that). If you hold 200+ investments, you are overinvested and overdiversified, and your results become mediocre at best.

To summarize, if you do not wish to spend too much time on this matter and want one simple recommendation, invest consistently in a broad equity index fund (but not a sector fund), and you will probably be ahead of 90–95% of investors in the long term.

It is hard to predict the future, but if your index fund is down after 10–15 years of your investment in it, all other non-index funds will probably be in much worse shape because of their higher operating expenses (i.e. the MER and commissions) and a high(er) portfolio turnover. Most financial institutions that sell mutual funds also offer index funds.

I want to emphasize that investing in mutual funds, especially equity mutual funds, is a risky venture, and 10 years from now you could have less money than when you invested it initially (similar to what happened in Japan: the Japanese stock market in 2014 was about 60% lower than at its peak in 1989–90).

The Dollar Cost Average strategy, i.e. investing on bi-weekly or monthly basis, lowers the risk of losing your capital. If the stock market goes down for many years, you buy more and more shares cheaper and cheaper, so when the market recovers, your investments will be worth more.

If your investment time horizon is less than 5 years (and assuming the rate of inflation is very low), do not invest in mutual funds at all.

In this case, the most important thing is the return OF your money rather than the return ON your money.

Segregated funds

Segregated funds are similar to mutual funds sold by financial institutions. They work in a similar way and include stocks and bonds. They have MERs, too.

MERs on segregated funds are higher than MERs of similar mutual funds, but segregated funds offer some unique features.

Segregated funds are sold by insurance companies only, and your investment is usually guaranteed (usually 75% or 100% of your invested amount) if you hold the investment for a certain period of time (typically 15 years).

A guarantee is provided by the insurance company that sells the funds to you, but in case the company fails, your investment is protected by Assuris at www.assuris.ca.

When the owner of the funds dies, the beneficiaries (designated by the owner before death) receive either the guaranteed death benefit or the market value, depending on which is higher.

There is no need for probate after death since the proceeds are paid directly to the beneficiaries. Money invested in segregated funds can be exempt from seizure (sometimes called creditor protection).

Another difference with segregated funds is not only are capital gains allocated to the fund holder, but capital losses are, too.

TIP 17
Segregated funds

If you buy a segregated fund, consider buying the riskiest one because if your investment is guaranteed, there is no need to be conservative.

You can gain much more when you choose the riskiest investment, but your loss is known in advance (e.g. if it is 75% guaranteed, then 75% of your initial investment is protected, and this is how much you will get back in the worst case scenario).

Chapter 3 notes

Please use this space for your notes.

Part 2: Liabilities

Hereafter, when I use the term "financial institution" (FI), it refers to any financial company that lends or collects money after providing a service and may check credit history (e.g. a finance company, a broker, a cell phone company, a car dealer, etc.).

A financial institution bases its decision to lend you money on several criteria:

- your credit history and/or relation with the bank (if there is any relationship and you are not a brand new client)

- debt and income ratios

- your income and work tenure

- your net worth (assets minus liabilities)

- collateral provided (if needed)

- your skin in the game (how much money you put down when, for example, you buy a car or a home)

In case you do not qualify for credit as a single applicant, financial institutions will consider a co-signer for your application. If you apply jointly with someone, the calculations and considerations will be the same. In other words, the bank will check the credit history of both applicants and will use the joint income, assets, and liabilities of both applicants.

Chapter 4: CREDIT HISTORY

Credit history is one of the criteria financial institutions want to see in good standing.

When you apply for credit, there are multiple considerations for the financial institution to either decline or approve you.

If your credit history is not so good, but you have a lot of assets and a very good income, financial institutions might still give you credit.

However, if you have a very good credit history, all the ratios are in order, and the income is stable but you had several inquiries on your credit history report from other financial institutions in the last month or two, your application might still be declined.

When applying for credit, financial institutions want to assess their risks and want to know what the likelihood of late payments or a complete credit write-off is. You have more chances to be approved and receive a lower interest on your loan or line of credit if this likelihood is low.

If you qualify for a mortgage, the interest on it usually does not depend on your credit history. Interest on credit cards is pre-determined, and you can only request to lower the rate when you are already a holder of the credit card.

Your credit history (or lack of it) will impact the decision of your banker whether or not to lend you money. The credit history is probably the most important decision factor.

Note that information regarding credit score or history is provided based on my observation and experience. Credit agencies might collect information and calculate scores somewhat differently in reality. It can be difficult to get reliable information about exactly how credit scores are calculated because credit agencies (Equifax and TransUnion) do not disclose that information.

Your credit file is created when you first borrow money or apply for credit.

There is a hit on your credit history report every time someone checks your credit history.

There are two types of hits: soft and hard.

- **Soft hits** happen when you open a bank account or buy a cell phone, for example. They check if you have any delinquency in the past; soft hits do not affect your credit score.

- **Hard hits** do affect your credit score. Every time you apply for credit and a financial institution runs your credit history (i.e. requests your credit report from a credit agency), a hard hit happens.

Credit reports consist of two things: **credit score** and **credit history.**

You personally can check your credit history as many times as you wish and it will not affect your score.

When you check your credit history, you get extra information, for example, how to improve your credit score. You can get your credit history report by snail mail for free.

You cannot get your credit score for free. If you need immediate access to your credit history report or credit score online, you will have to pay. Please consult specific agencies' websites to obtain more information.

There are two primary credit agencies in Canada:

- www.equifax.ca

- www.transunion.ca

You can also call Equifax at 1–800–465-7166 or TransUnion at 1–800–663-9980.

Even though credit history reports issued by different agencies may have approximately the same information, the calculated scores will most likely be somewhat different.

TIP 18
Credit history privacy measure

Credit account numbers you have in your credit history reports might have slightly different account numbers than in reality because some companies want to protect their clients from fraud and so report account numbers with one or two different digits or letters or with one or two missing digits or letters.

Your credit history shows:

- your payment patterns

- how many late payments or collections or bankruptcies you have had

- how much debt you have and with which company

- balances above their limits

- what "job" you have

- any alerts, e.g. telephone number or your legal name that does not match credit agencies' records

- how many times you have applied for different credit accounts in the last 12 months

- how long you have lived or worked at the same place

It does not usually show authorized overdraft (even if your account was overdrawn at the time your credit history was checked).

In many cases it does not show your mortgage(s) (but will show your Home Equity Line of Credit).

Many records regarding your credit accounts stay in your credit history report for many years (I have seen 20 years+). However, they become less important and relevant as time passes.

Your credit score is a summary of your credit history in one number; the higher the number, the better the credit history.

Credit score incorporates the following:

- number of inquiries

- paying bills on time

- credit utilization

- payment history and credit time length

- types of credit: revolving (e.g. credit cards), open (e.g. cell phone contracts), or installment (e.g. loans)

Credit report agencies Equifax and TransUnion use a scale from 300 to 900.

One of the most important things that will impact your credit score is the number of inquiries (hard hits), i.e. how many times you have applied for different types of credit in the last 12 months.

Financial institutions often decline applicants just because they have several hard hits in their credit history report within a short period of time (1–6 months).

Each time a person applies for credit, credit score points are lost. Moreover, when a few applications are submitted within a short period of time, each additional application will remove more points than the previous ones.

Example: Multiple credit checks

Mr. X wants to borrow money and he goes to three different financial institutions: FI A, FI B and FI C. Each FI will check X's credit history, and the following hits occur to his credit score:

- When he applies with FI A, he loses 5 points from his credit score.

- The next day he applies for credit with FI B, and he loses 10 points (regardless of whether or not FI A approves him).

- The next day Mr. X applies with FI C, and this time he loses 50 points.

- The more an individual applies for credit within a short period of time, the more risk the system sees in the application and she or he will start to lose points exponentially.

However, some financial institutions make an exception when clients apply for a mortgage: their credit history check might result in a soft hit, which will not affect the credit score.

TIP 19
Limit your credit checks

Try not just to avoid FIs' inquiries about your credit history but ask specifically not to run it if it is not necessary (e.g. when you need to increase the limit on your credit card, you can intentionally ask the credit card company not to check your credit history from credit agencies).

If you do not ask that, they will probably run your credit history report. However, in many cases they can increase the limit based on your repayment history with them.

If a person applies for a mortgage and the financial institution assures them that it will be a soft hit, they can go to another FI, too, and be certain that they will not be declined due to a previous hard hit.

The utilization ratio is very important for your credit score. Consider the following two examples with two different credit cards.

Example: Credit capacity

Compare these two scenarios:

- You have a $1,000 credit card balance (a "balance" is what you already spent) and the credit card limit is $1,000.

- You have a $1,000 credit card balance on your credit card and a limit of $5,000.

The difference is that in the first example the person spent 100% of money available to them (the utilization ratio is 100%), and in the second case the person spent only 20% of the available money (the utilization ratio is 20%). Financial institutions do not know why the person spent 100% in the first case.

Perhaps this individual spends $1,000 per month, and it was not related to how much available credit they have, or alternatively, perhaps this individual always spends up to the max of the available credit they have, no matter what the maximum is.

Obviously, if the utilization ratio is lower, banks will have more trust in the card holder. The utilization ratio should not exceed 30%, no matter what the available limit on the credit card is. It is better to have three cards with $330 balance and $1,000 limits on each card rather than one card with $990 balance and $1,000 limit.

It is very bad if the balance on your credit facility (e.g. credit card, overdraft, line of credit) is higher than the limit (e.g. the Visa balance is $1,050 but the limit is only $1,000). This thing alone can be the reason to decline your credit application.

TIP 20
Look at your own credit history

If you apply for credit, ask in advance if you would be able to see your credit history, too.

You might not get a paper copy (the policy of some financial institutions might not allow it), but there shouldn't be any problem for you to at least view it.

Avoid clerks who do not want to share your credit history with you. It is your credit history, after all, and you have the right to see it. This is especially important if the application is declined, since that happens mostly due to credit history. Unfortunately, clerks who process the application (e.g. car dealers) do not always have access to your credit report because they do not check your credit history themselves; it is done by the FI that they deal with.

Information about you is reported to credit agencies, and they know your full legal name, SIN, address, telephone, company where you work, etc. They have an idea of how much you should be making annually (if you are an employee) based on the place where you work. Based on this they "know" how much debt is too much for you.

In many cases, your credit report might have alerts indicating if your SIN or name or telephone or address is incorrect.

Your credit report may contain mistakes (e.g. instead of Smith they may have Simith; your SIN may not be entirely correct), or they might have out-dated information (e.g. in case you moved to another address or got married).

If information is wrong, it is (unfortunately) your responsibility to fix it. You can contact the credit agency in writing and provide proof of the correct information, or you can ask the bank or credit union you are dealing with if they can submit a request to the credit agency to fix the mistake.

Mistakes are frequent, in particular if the parent and child living in the same household have the same first or middle and last names. The parent's credit history may reflect (some of) the credit history of the child and vice versa.

This must be fixed because when you apply for credit, banks do not care why you have this much debt and do not accept explanations that these debts belong to your parent or child.

If your credit report has incorrect information, such as collections, most of the time this has to be corrected by the financial institution you had (or did not have) a problem or collection with. The credit agencies will probably not accept any faxes or letters with explanations from you (i.e. a letter of direction).

Simply ask the financial institution to fix your credit report directly.

If you had collections or any other issues with your credit history, and you paid the debt off or fixed the problems, never throw away your proof. Even after 10 years, banks might ask for them when you apply for credit.

From the credit score point of view, it might be a good idea to have at least a couple of different credit cards. However, if you have only one credit card with a long (at least one year), good repayment history and no late payments on it, it should be enough, and your credit score should be good enough.

The longer the history of your credit account, the more impact it has on your score: e.g. if you received a new credit card 3 months ago it will have less impact on your credit score than your older credit card which you have had for 10 years.

Your credit score might change several times a day, not necessarily once a month.

It might go up or down, depending on the activity in your credit history (e.g. if you just paid a bill your credit score goes up because of the utilization ratio; when you apply for credit your score goes down because there was a hit on your credit history).

In other words, whatever your score is at the moment, it does not necessarily mean that it will stay that way forever.

If you check your credit score with credit report agencies, you get plenty of information on how to improve it, what score you have, and why you have that score.

Some information may not be in your credit history report, but financial institutions pay attention to it. If you just recently moved (or recently changed your work) and your new address or work is not yet reported in the credit history, it will have a (slight) negative impact on your credit application.

Also note that banks prefer stability, so they would like you to live in one place without moving every year or two.

Banks usually pay more attention to the credit history than to the credit score (some banks even do not have access to your credit score, just credit history).

If you apply for a car loan with a dealership, they usually care less about how much debt you have, but they do pay attention to how good your repayment history is.

They also often care more about your credit score rather than your credit history.

Tips to optimize your credit history

1. First of all, you need to know what you have on your credit history report. It might be a good idea to run it on your own before applying for any type of credit. When you check your credit history on your own, it does not affect your credit history or score. If you have bad credit history and you do not know about that, your credit score will become even worse after applying for credit (because of the hard hit when a financial institution checks your credit score).

2. If you have outstanding collections, pay them off. Nobody will lend you money if you have unpaid collections. Keep all proofs of payments forever.

3. If you have late payments in the last 24 months, you need to have a good explanation why you were late. Nobody will lend you money if you say that you simply decided to postpone the payment for a month or two or did not have the money.

4. If you have a bad credit score because your credit cards are over the limit (and the score might be very bad just because of that reason alone), increase the limit. Keep in mind that you will have to bring your balance below the limit to begin with, before credit card companies would even consider increasing your limit.

5. If you had several inquiries of your credit history by different financial institutions in the last 2–3 months, wait for a few months before you apply for credit again.

6. Your utilization ratio should not exceed 30–35% of the limit of your credit card or line of credit.

7. Do not be late with your bill payments. Always pay them 2–3 days before due date.

Note: Even when you have a bad credit history, you may still qualify for credit if you bring a strong co-signer. Even if you had bankruptcy, you will be able to get a loan or credit card with a strong co-signer. A strong co-signer is a person with good credit history, assets, high stable income, and not much debt.

If you must apply with a co-signer, in order for the credit to appear on your credit history report, you should be the primary applicant and have your co-signer as the secondary one.

It does not matter to a bank who is the primary and who is the secondary co-signer (because for your bank you are both equally responsible no matter how it is reported to credit agencies), but in many cases banks report only the primary applicant to the credit agencies. If you are the secondary applicant, it might not appear on your credit history report, and it will not help your credit history.

Note: The financial industry distinguishes between "good debt" (money that you borrow to buy an appreciating asset) and "bad debt" (money that you borrow to buy a depreciating asset). Never ask your banker which debt is good or bad because for your banker every debt that you borrow and pay interest on is good. If you need to borrow, consider how much debt you can afford rather than how much debt you are approved for.

Some pitfalls to be aware of

Some financial institutions do not keep clients' credit history on file even for a short period of time. If you apply for credit and the FI needs to modify your application or makes another application (e.g. you do not qualify on your own and you have to bring a co-signer, so the FI creates a new credit application), they will have to run your credit history again. This does affect your credit history in a negative way because of the hard hits explained above.

Unfortunately, there is nothing you can do to avoid these double hits because you give your consent to run your credit history, and the FI does not necessarily keep its clients' credit history.

You can definitely inquire if they run the credit history again before applying the second time, but even if this is the case, you cannot do much about it if you want to get credit. Going to another FI will not help because another FI will run your credit history, too, and you will have a hard hit again.

Financial institutions often run a credit history without considering how it will affect the client. I know of a case where a person wanted to lease a car from a car dealer, and his credit history was run four times in the same day. You can imagine what score this customer had after that.

Ratios used for borrowing qualifications

Banks do not care how much money you make and how much debt you have as long as the ratios are in order (from my observations, phone companies or car dealers do not calculate ratios, but they want to see the credit repayment history in good shape and want to confirm the applying individual has income).

Many people think that if a person is a co-borrower for someone's debt, banks will divide this debt by two to know each person's debt share. This is not the case. Banks do not care if you are the only person responsible for debt or if you are a co-signer with someone else.

Typically, the most useful and used ratio for banks is TDS (Total Debt Service ratio).

Your TDS ratio is your monthly payments (see below) divided by your gross monthly income (i.e. income before tax; if you are self employed, gross income is income after expenses but before tax).

Some banks might calculate it a little bit differently, but the idea is the same.

Monthly payments are:

Debt that appears on your credit history report:

- 3% of the outstanding balance of your credit cards

- 2.5% of the limit (not balance) of your line of credit

- loan payments (e.g. car loan, student loan, mortgage)

- vehicle lease payment

- last cell phone payment from the credit history report

- other outstanding debt payments

Additional monthly payments that usually do not appear on your credit history report (but which should be considered for credit application):

- rent (if you rent)

- property tax (if you own a place)

- heating (but not electricity)

- 50% (only) of condo fees (if you own a condo)

- alimony or child support payments

Example: Apartment rent

If you rent an apartment for $600 where utilities are included, and you have outstanding $450 on your credit card and owe $700 on your line of credit with a limit of $10,000, your monthly payment calculation is as follows:

($600 + $450 x 0.03 + $10,000 x 0.025) = $863.50

Banks do not care about your personal insurance, telephone bills (if they are not on your credit history), electricity, and other expenses.

The cut-off point for the TDS ratio is about 40–42% for most of the banks.

If your TDS is above 40% (meaning more than 40% of your income goes toward the debt payments), banks do not like that but there might be exceptions based on other factors.

Banks do take into consideration how much total exposure to credit card debt you have (e.g. consider situations when the Visa limit is $10,000 but the outstanding balance is only $450), but they usually do not use it in their ratio calculation.

**TIP 21
Pay off the highest-interest debt first**

Many people who have several types of credit (credit cards, loans, mortgages) tend to first pay off the debt with the highest balance although the interest might not be the highest on that debt. That is not a wise strategy.

Your first priority should be to get rid of the debt which has the highest interest, regardless of the balance.

Example: Total Debt Service Calculation

These assume that the individual has good credit history in both cases. Which person will be more easily approved for credit, based on the TDS ratio?

1. A person with only one credit card and $500 balance on it, paying the monthly rent of $300, utilities included, and having the monthly income of $1,000.

2. The TDS ratio is 31.5%: (3% of $500+$300)/$1,000. (No heating added because the rent includes utilities.)

3. Another person with $600 car loan, $1,200 monthly mortgage payment, $200 property tax and income of $3,750 per month.

The TDS ratio is 53.3%+: ($600+$1,200+$200+heating)/$3,750. (In this case heating has to be added because this person pays for it.)

The individual from the first example has a better chance to be approved for credit.

Income

If you are an employee, the bank uses your monthly salary (or will calculate it if you are paid per hour).

If you are self-employed or a contractor, the bank wants to see you as self-employed for at least 2 years and uses the lowest income (i.e. total income minus total expenses but before taxes) of the last 2 years divided by 12 (months).

Your other sources of income might be: pension, CPP/OAS, alimony, investment income (usually when it is consistent over the last 2–3 years), employment bonuses and/or commissions (consistent over the last 2–3 years), RRIF payments, permanent disability, and scholarship.

Not everything that you would consider an income will qualify for credit application.

Some income that will not qualify is: unemployment, welfare, loans, government child benefit, parent child support, RRSP withdrawal, casual insurance payments, and income that you pay to yourself from your own company (if less than for 2–3 years).

Banks might consider your income if you are on a leave (e.g. maternity leave) and if you can prove that your company will rehire you.

Banks only care about your current income and will usually not consider future bonuses, increases in salary, etc.

Assets

Assets are what you own which may appreciate in value and/or yield income (e.g. rental property, business, investment portfolio).

There are two types of assets: liquid and illiquid.

- Liquid assets are assets that you can literally sell within 24 hours and get cash (savings accounts, GICs, stocks, etc.).

- Illiquid assets are assets that would take time to sell, and their exact value is not known until you sell them (vehicles, real estate, etc.).

Banks would rather lend money to a person who has only $50,000 in non-registered mutual funds (liquid assets) than to a person who owns only a $200,000 house (illiquid assets), everything else being equal.

Liabilities

Every debt (even deferred debt, such as a student loan) costs money.

Obviously, the less debt you have the better your financial situation is.

It is usually difficult to find interest-free liabilities, so by avoiding liabilities you save your time that you would spend working to pay the interest.

Something to consider: Interest you see on your liabilities statements is what you have to pay after you have paid your income tax.

Example: The real interest you pay

If you make $60,000 per year, your tax bracket is 32%. If you have a credit card charging 19.99% annually, the 19.99% interest is AFTER you have paid your income tax, so you do not pay your interest out of $60,000 but out of (about) $40,000 that you have after tax. To put it differently, your real interest on the credit card then becomes 30%+ BEFORE you have paid your income tax.

When you apply for credit, banks would like your net worth to be positive (i.e. you own more assets than you owe debts).

You do not know the exact value of your assets until you sell them. The value of your assets will fluctuate up and down. Your debt will not fluctuate; you know it at any given time.

Collateral

Most lending provided by banks is unsecured (except mortgages).

However, if there is a risk that the borrower will not pay off the debt, financial institutions use security (collateral). In case that happens, the FI will take (and sell) the collateral.

Some of the assets can be used as collateral (e.g. non-registered GICs or mutual funds, vehicles, real estate, cash value of life insurance), while some cannot (e.g. RRSP).

When collateral is involved, it (often) has to be registered (so the asset cannot be sold until the debt is paid off) and the borrower pays for its registration.

In some cases, the borrower might not even know their asset has been held as collateral until they try to sell the asset and cannot do that. If the debt was paid in full, the title of the asset should be changed and the lien removed.

TIP 22
Waive collateral

Always ask if the financial institution can waive the collateral registration fee, since they can often do that when asked.

Many banks "forget" to do that until the client asks them to. (For example, if you buy a car from a dealer or take a loan from your bank, the loan or financing will be approved with the vehicle registration as collateral without you being told about this explicitly).

When banks use collateral, this obviously reduces the overall risk to the bank, but unfortunately, it usually does not reduce the interest of the credit.

Banks will not lend you money based on collateral alone, they use a variety of criteria, including your income, assets, and credit history.

Chapter 4 notes

Please use this space for your notes.

Chapter 5: CREDIT ACCOUNTS

Credit cards, credit lines, and overdrafts are called revolving debt (you can pay just the interest during each payment period, and you "re-use" these accounts again and again).

Loans (including mortgages) are called non-revolving debt because you cannot re-use them. Once you pay them off, you must apply for a new loan.

Applicants must have reached the age of majority in their province or territory of residence before they apply for credit.

Overdraft

Overdraft is a feature associated with chequing or savings accounts that allows you to borrow up to an allowed limit (below zero on your account balance).

Usually banks charge for overdraft protection (though its cost might be included in premium accounts). Sometimes you have overdraft protection and also pay "as you go" which means that if you use it, the bank charges you a fee and interest for the period your account was overdrawn. If you do not use the overdraft, you do not pay any fees.

Usually, your account is not allowed to be overdrawn for more than 30 days in a row. Typical annual interest for overdraft is 21%.

If you do not have overdraft on your account (i.e. you haven't applied for an overdraft and haven't been approved for it) and you have a very good relationship with your bank, the bank might allow your account to be overdrawn for a small amount of money (the so-called courtesy overdraft). However, do not count on it because this privilege can be taken away at any moment.

TIP 23
Overdraft and bouncing cheques

Banks do not like surprises.
You can negotiate many things and ask for many exceptions if you notify your bank in advance before something happens to your bank account.
For example, if you find out that you do not have enough money in your account, but you wrote a cheque and you need it to be honoured, advise your bank and they might help you (for example, by giving you a temporary overdraft). If you do not advise them, it is likely that the cheque will bounce, and it will impact your relationship with your bank in the future.

Credit cards

There are several types of credit cards:

- prepaid cards
- gift cards
- regular secured or unsecured credit cards

Prepaid credit cards and gift cards do not establish or maintain your credit history (i.e. they are not reported to the credit agencies).

Prepaid cards

Prepaid cards can be loaded with any amount of money and used until you have spent all the money. In some cases they can be re-loaded again. There are only a few credit card companies that offer this type of credit card.

Gift cards

Gift cards are usually good for only one load (typically up to $500). After you have spent all the money on it, you throw it away. Many stores and some banks offer gift credit cards. Gift cards have a one-time activation fee of a few dollars. You can check the remaining balance on the credit card by calling customer service or check it online using the website of the credit card company.

Regular (secured and unsecured) credit cards

If you have a relatively low income, it is easier to qualify or get a credit card from a department store than from a credit card company or a bank. Department stores (or more precisely, credit card issuers that they deal with) usually rely on your previous repayment history, and they care less about your debt ratios (as explained above).

Your credit card bill has several important parts:

- **Balance**: This is the outstanding amount you owe to the credit card company (i.e. money you have spent + interest + other charges during the month).

- **Credit card limit**: This is the maximum amount that you can spend. Your balance should be less than the limit. You can usually exceed the limit by a small amount (usually up to 10% of the limit), but it is bad for your credit history, and you are charged an over-limit fee for that (but if you bring the balance below the limit before the statement is issued, you will not be charged the over-limit fee). Most credit cards in Canada have credit limits. Those that do not must be paid off in full every month.

- **Due date**: This is the date by which your credit card company has to receive the minimum payment.

- **Minimum payment**: This is the amount which you absolutely have to pay by the due date, in order for your credit history to be in good standing.

- **Interest**: This is the annual percent you will pay in case you do not pay your balance in full by the due date. The interest can vary depending on the credit card company.

Note: The maximum annual interest rate allowed under the Criminal Code is 60% per year). If you have several late payments during the year, the credit card company may increase your interest. A typical credit card interest in Canada is between 18.99% and 29.99%.

How do credit cards work?

When you have a credit card, you have 30 days to use it and usually 21 days afterwards to pay your bill, i.e. you have 51 days to use your credit card company's money.

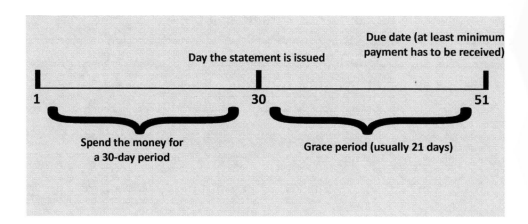

- The 21-day period is called a "grace period" and the 30-day period is called a "billing cycle."

- As long as you respect the due date, credit card companies do not care if you pay your bill right after you receive it, or just 2 days before it is due. As long as they get at least the minimum payment by the due date, your credit history will not be affected (but keep in mind the utilization ratio explained above). Make sure you pay your credit card bill at least 2 days before the due date because it takes a couple of days for your credit card company to receive the money.

- If you do not pay your balance in full by the due date, you will have to pay interest starting from the day of the first purchase of the billing cycle. You will never pay any interest if you pay your balance in full every month by the due date.

- If you withdraw a cash advance (i.e. you take money out from your credit card up to your credit card limit), you will pay interest starting from the day you withdraw it. There is no grace period on cash advance. The interest on a cash advance is usually higher than the regular interest on your credit card carrying balance. Many credit card companies charge an extra fee for using cash advance, too.

Secured credit cards

Secured credit cards are issued by banks and credit card companies. Many banks do not offer secured cards.

Your security (collateral) is typically a GIC that you hold at your bank. Your credit card limit is usually equal to the value of the provided collateral. You pay your credit card bill every month (if there is any balance), and your collateral is used only if you do not pay your bill at all. You do not need to pay your balance in full, just the minimum, but similar to regular credit cards, you will be charged interest if you do not pay it in full.

Upon return or cancellation of the credit card, you will get your collateral back. Sometimes you can ask to remove the collateral after a certain period of time and after the credit card company reviews your repayment history.

Most banks and credit card companies do not give credit cards if you are not a Canadian permanent resident or citizen of Canada, even on a secured basis. However, exceptions are possible, for example, if you are an international student or a foreign employee with a high salary and a valid work permit.

Most credit cards issued in Canada are unsecured.

Benefits of credit cards

There are several good reasons to use credit cards. Many credit cards offer benefits that will save you money. Some credit cards are free to use, while others have an annual fee.

Note that interest and an annual fee are two separate things: you might have a free credit card but you will still pay interest if you do not pay the balance in full every month.

This credit card website at http://artemfinancial.ca/links/credit-cards-site compares some (but not all) Canadian credit card deals.

- Some cards offer points you can redeem, or cash back. These options are very popular among Canadians. The idea is that you get a certain percentage back of what you spend monthly or annually. Points that you receive from one credit card company are not necessarily the same points you will get by using another credit card company, even if both companies call them points.

- Some cards might give you an extra bonus in the form of points or a cash back bonus, or waive interest for a certain period of time.

- Many credit cards offer valuable insurance or coverage, such as travel insurance, rent-a-car insurance, trip interruption, or trip cancellation.

- Many credit cards offer extended warranty (for up to two years) which automatically doubles the original manufacturer's warranty of most personal items you purchase.

Note: Many people do not understand why they get all these benefits for free in addition to the grace period. The reason is simple: every time you pay with your card, the business you paid with your credit card has to pay the credit card company (usually 1–2% of the transaction). So the service is free for you, but it is not free to the businesses you buy from.

If you are not a Skilled Worker immigrant, some banks might issue a secured credit card for you.

If you do not have credit history, do not apply for a credit card with a department store because you will probably be declined.

If you do not have credit history at all, but you want to establish it without applying for a credit card, you can sign a contract (usually 2 years) with a cell phone company. Do not buy a cell phone that you have to prepay, since this type of contract will not help you to build a credit history.

Some disadvantages of using credit cards

- Your credit card information can be compromised, and you might be a victim of a fraud or identity theft.

- The credit card company and many of its employees will know what you bought. Your purchases will be known to the credit card company and perhaps even to third parties.

- If you have a joint card holder, they will also know how you spend your money.

Do not use credit cards if you do not want anybody to know what you bought. Use gift credit cards instead, since they do not bear your name and can be used anonymously.

Credit card promotions

Sometimes credit card companies offer cash advance options with low interest for a certain period of time. To use the promotion, you get cheques from the company, which you can use to pay off other debts (or, if the promo interest plus the fees are less than your bank's savings account interest, you can deposit the promotion cheques in your savings account to earn some money).

You do not get these cheques automatically, but you have to call the credit card company and ask them to send you these promo cheques (as per the government's strict regulations).

If you receive cheques from your credit card company with a number of different promotions, it is a good idea to know some of the pitfalls before you write a cheque.

Example 1: 0% cheque offer

You receive a cheque offering a 0% annual rate but a 1% fee of the transferred balance for a certain period of time. However, some credit card companies may charge a regular cash advance interest on this fee.

For example, you receive a cheque with this kind of offer expiring in 6 months. You write a $10,000 cheque, and the credit card company charges you a $100 fee (1% of $10,000), but the next month they may charge you 19.99% annual interest on this $100, claiming that paying this fee was a regular cash advance transaction which falls outside their promo offer.

Example 2: Cheap cash advance

You receive a cheque offering a 2% fee on cash advance, with the offer expiring in 3 months.

Many customers will think that this means it is a 2% annual interest offer and will be tempted to accept the offer. However, the 2% fee actually translates into 8% annual interest (2% times four 3-month periods).

Example 3: Promotion cheque

You receive a 0% interest promo cheque. Your current outstanding balance before writing a cheque is $5,000.

You decide to use the promo cheque and write a cheque for $10,000. The next month, when you receive your statement, your outstanding balance is $15,000, and you decide to pay off $6,000.

The payment will not go towards the balance with the highest interest first, but your payment will be adjusted proportionally, i.e. 2/3 of the payment will go towards $10,000 (and you will pay 0% interest on the remaining $6,000) and 1/3 will go towards the initial $5,000 (and you will pay your regular interest on the remaining $3,000).

If you want to use these promo cheques:

- make sure you do not owe anything on this card at the time you write the cheque

- make sure that you do not expect to use the card during the promo period (because that would gather extra interest)

Example 4: Promotion errors

Unfortunately, credit card companies may make mistakes with promotions. For example, let's say that you receive a cheque with a promotion in January. You do not use it and it expires in several months. In September you receive another cheque with another promotion, and you decide to use it. This new promo cheque may bear the same cheque number as the one in January, so when you use it, the credit card company might accidentally treat your September cheque as the January cheque.

Since the January promo has already expired, this will count as regular cash advance and you will pay regular interest, rather than the September promo rate. Pay attention to extra fees, and if you do not anticipate a particular fee, always ask your credit card company about it.

Do not assume that credit card companies do not make mistakes.

Authorized users on your credit cards

You can ask your credit card company to issue an additional card called an "authorized user" card. It is not the same as a joint co-applicant of your credit card. It will not affect the credit history of the other person (authorized user), and it will not appear on his or her credit report. This individual can also be under 18 years old. With some credit card companies, you can ask for the authorized user to have a different card limit, e.g. lower than your credit card limit so you can give it to your child to use.

By default, you will not receive two separate bills, but your credit card bill will show your transactions and those of the authorized user separately. However, you may ask the credit card company to issue two separate transaction statements. An authorized user is not permitted to get any information if they call customer service.

Some credit card companies offer Visa debit cards. In Canada, they are usually used as debit cards, but they are also often accepted in lieu of credit cards, in particular overseas and for online purchases.

TIP 24
Borrowing to invest

Borrowing to invest has a lot of risk: your investment can drop in value, but you will still owe the same amount of debt. Remember that since your asset value is based on what other people are ready to pay for it, it will always fluctuate in value. On the other hand, your debt is constant and you know how much you owe at any given point in time.

If you borrow to invest in an RRSP, you can pay off your RRSP loan (at least partially) with a refund you may get from the CRA (you will get a refund if you paid more taxes than you should be paying). When you borrow to invest in non-registered investments, you will not get any refund and your loan interest might not be deductible in future years (it might be deductible only if the investment you buy has a potential to generate income; see more details in investment section).

Unfortunately, your advisor might have a conflict of interest. Advice from different advisors may differ (please visit http://artemfinancial.ca/links/ethic-finance to learn about ethics in the financial industry). If you disregard my recommendation and still want to borrow to invest – do so when there is a panic in the market. Never ever borrow to invest when the market has been up for several years, and everybody is happy about the returns. The price you pay for your investment is very important.

When you use Visa debit cards, the money is taken from the corresponding account instantly.

You do not have to have a credit history to get a Visa debit card, and it does not establish your credit history. However, it is a very convenient option if you do not qualify for a regular credit card or just do not want one. Visa debit cards are still relatively new in Canada, and not all banks or credit card companies have this product.

Loans

Similar to credit cards, loans can be secured or unsecured. Most secured loans are given for vehicle purchases (and the same vehicle is used as the bank's collateral). Usually banks give loans for 36–60 months, and brand new vehicle loans can be extended to up to 84 months. Loans are paid off via regular payments which consist of interest plus the principal (i.e. part of the borrowed amount), at least once a month.

In some rare cases, installments can be "interest only," but those loans are usually investment loans.

If your loan is unsecured and you want to reduce interest on it, you can ask your bank to secure it (by GIC, mutual fund, vehicle or another asset). Banks do not offer that themselves, but if the amount is substantial, banks might accept collateral and reduce the interest.

Interest charged for loans is typically between 5% (very good clients) and 15% (high risk clients). The interest can be fixed or variable (see below). If you apply for a car loan with a dealer, they might charge you much more than 15% (make sure to read the fine print in your contract). The interest is simple (i.e. not compound).

Banks might increase your interest if you have late payments on your loan.

Loans that banks offer are typically open loans: you can repay them at any time without any penalty. You can also increase your payments to any amount or make an extra payment at any time.

If you have debt in different banks or credit card debt, it is a good idea to consolidate all the debts with a loan. In this case, banks usually do not allow you to keep the accounts you want to consolidate, i.e. you will have to close them.

Consolidating your debt should not affect your credit history in a negative way. There is no difference in your credit history report between a regular loan and a consolidation loan. The consolidation loan does not reduce your credit score per se (unless it is forced by a bank due to late payments on other debts).

There are two types of interest rates: fixed and variable. You have the choice of which interest rate you choose when you apply for a loan.

- A fixed interest rate is set for the whole term of the loan (up to 5 years), and it will not change. If the loan term is longer than 5 years, the interest has to be renegotiated again at maturity after 5 years.

- A variable interest rate depends on the prime rate, and your interest may fluctuate. However, your regular payments are normally fixed (they do not change during the term of the loan up to 5 years), and what will change is the number of these payments. If the prime rate goes down, you will have fewer payments (since more of each payment will go towards the principal); if the prime rate goes up, you will have more payments to make (since more of each payment goes towards the interest). The payment should always cover the interest at least, so if the prime rate goes up too high and the payment falls short of covering the interest, it will be adjusted by the bank.

TIP 25
Considering a car loan with a dealer

Some dealers sell cars with (close to) 0% interest, but they increase their price to compensate. Ask your dealer what the cost of the same vehicle would be if you paid cash. The price might be significantly lower. In this case, you can ask your bank for a car loan, and it might be cheaper to pay your bank's interest than buy the "interest free" car from that dealer.

TIP 26
RRSP loan

If you contribute to an RRSP consistently, it might be a good idea to take an RRSP loan just before you file your income tax at the beginning of the next calendar year, to minimize your interest payment on the loan. Refunds usually arrive within 3–4 weeks after filing your tax report, and once your refund arrives, you can use it to pay off the RRSP loan, in which case your interest payment on the RRSP loan will be relatively small.

For example, you contribute $7,000 during the year and take an RRSP loan of $3,000 in February of the next year. If your tax bracket is 32%, you will get a $3,200 refund with which you can pay off the RRSP loan in full. Now you do not have an outstanding RRSP loan, and the value of your RRSP is ~$10,000.

TIP 27
Dealer's loan details

When you compare dealership financing vs. bank loans, make sure that the same conditions apply: the type of interest (variable/fixed), the type of financing or loan (secured/unsecured), and the amortization period.

In many cases, you might think you are getting a much cheaper vehicle financing with a dealer because you haven't looked at the conditions closely enough, but you may actually do better through your bank.

Fixed interest rates are usually higher than variable rates, everything else being equal. Most loans in Canada have variable interest.

Many people take RRSP loans (whether or not you should contribute to an RRSP at all is another story, see the RRSP section). It might be a good idea to contribute to an RRSP if your income or tax bracket is high. If you take an RRSP loan and invest with the same bank, they usually offer you a very low rate, close to the prime interest. Among things to consider is how much you will save if you pay, say, 5% interest on an RRSP loan but get 32% back from the CRA (if your marginal tax rate is 32%). Keep in mind that you cannot deduct interest on this loan from your income.

I find the Ernst & Young calculator site (http://artemfinancial. ca/links/tax-calculators) very informative: it provides you with information about your tax and tax bracket based on your income and province or territory of residence.

Certain banks and investment companies offer investment loans for high net-worth clients. Obviously, financial institutions that lend you money want you to invest in their mutual funds and GICs; they may even refuse to lend if you do not wish to invest in their investment products. In many cases, interest on investment loans is low, and sometimes loans are interest only loans (you will pay off the principal in the future when your asset appreciates in value).

You can deduct interest when you borrow money to invest in a non-registered investment, i.e. you buy income producing investments: interest or dividends. Please consult a knowledgeable accountant as the CRA does not like investment loans for their tax deductibility, and it is very important to get professional advice before you proceed with an investment loan.

You can have life and disability insurance on a loan (see explanation about this in the insurance section).

Credit lines

A credit line is a revolving credit account.

You can borrow up to the credit line limit as many times as you wish. Banks oblige you to pay at least the interest on a monthly basis, and it is largely up to you when you want to pay off the principal, if at all. Interest is simple.

Example: Simple interest

Simple interest is calculated as follows:

(outstanding balance /365 days) x interest x (number of days you borrow the money for)

For example, let's say that you owe $3,000, your interest is 6%, and the current month has 31 days. The interest that you owe this month is calculated as follows:

($3,000/365) x 0.06 x 31 = $15.29.

The calculation is based on the number of days you borrow the money for, so if you pay off the balance in full within 10 days, you just need to replace 31 days with 10 days in the formula (and would only pay $4.93 interest).

The interest on credit lines is always variable (i.e. not fixed). Everything else being equal, interest on a credit line is usually higher than on a loan, by default.

If you have debt and you wish to apply for a line of credit to consolidate the existing debt, banks will not allow you to do that (since lines of credit are revolving credits). However, if you already have a line of credit, you can use it to consolidate your debt.

You can have life and disability insurance on a line of credit.

TIP 28
Lower interest for larger loans

Some banks offer discounts if the amount of the loan you apply for exceeds a particular threshold. For example, if you ask to borrow $9,000, which the bank approves with a particular interest rate, you may ask the bank whether the interest will be lower if they increase the loan to $10,000. If the interest is indeed lower, ask to increase the loan to $10,000 and pay off $1,000 right away after you have received the loan.

There would be no penalty since the loans are usually open. Your monthly payment will be a little higher than if you took $9,000, but the interest will be lower. Usually the thresholds for interest rate discounts are in increments of $10,000 or $15,000 (i.e. $10,000, $25,000, $30,000, etc.).

Student loans or lines of credit

If you are a student (full time or part time) you can apply for a student loan or line of credit. Most students take student lines of credit from banks and student loans from the government.

The interest on student lines of credit is very low (usually, prime + 1%).

For certain lucrative professions, most banks offer professional lines of credit with an even lower interest. As for student loans, you often do not need to pay any interest on them until you graduate (plus 1 or 2 years after that).

One or two years after you graduate, your student loan or line of credit becomes a regular loan.

Getting qualified for a student line of credit

To qualify for credit, you often need to have a co-signer because banks want to be sure that you will be able to pay interest on it while you are at school. If you worked before you go to school and plan to continue to work while at school, banks will use your current or future income. Otherwise, you will need a co-signer with good income and good credit history to strengthen the application.

If you go to study for certain elite professions (like doctors, lawyers, accountants), banks will use your projected future income after you graduate, and you usually do not need a co-signer.

Chapter 5 notes

Please use this space for your notes.

Chapter 6: MORTGAGES

The biggest debt you (will) probably have is your mortgage. Up until recently mortgages were not the same as secured loans, but some banks started to change their policy to "lock" their clients. When you buy a house, it is very important to understand the difference between a mortgage and a loan (that is given to purchase a house).

A **collateral charge** (i.e. loan) is non-transferable. It cannot be switched to a new lender like a regular mortgage. Even if a bank gives you a loan to buy a house, they still call it a mortgage! If you are considering a collateral charge (i.e. loan), not a conventional charge (mortgage), have a mortgage professional explain the pros and cons before you jump in.

For regular mortgages, all of the main rules and conditions can be found in a land title document, which will be registered with your provincial land title or registry office. For collateral mortgages, rules and conditions are found in a loan agreement, which is registered differently. The article at the end of this book explains the difference.

Collateral loan agreements include terms that other lenders do not know of and may find unacceptable. For that and other reasons, lenders do not transfer from borrowers with collateral charges.

Please read the article "Beware the pitfalls of collateral mortgages" at the end of this book.

Most mortgages in Canada are variable or fixed rate mortgages (a very small portion of mortgages is a mix of these two rates and not all lenders offer them, but these are not discussed in this book).

Variable and fixed rate mortgages can be **closed** or **open**.

Note: Comparing fixed and variable mortgage payments with all other conditions equal (the same interest, term, amortization), payments on a fixed mortgage are smaller than payments on a variable mortgage.

| Advantages (+) and Disadvantages (-) of closed and open mortgages ||
Open mortgage (fixed or variable)	Closed mortgage (fixed or variable)
+No penalty to pay off the mortgage off or any portion of it +Mortgage can be switched to another lender or renewed to any mortgage with the current lender at any time with no cost -Interest rate is higher than a similar term or type closed mortgage	+Interest rate is lower than a similar term or type open mortgage -Penalty has to be paid if renewed, transferred or paid off prior to maturity (banks allow to renew closed mortgages 90 or 120 days prior to maturity without any penalty)

| Advantages (+) and Disadvantages (-) of fixed and variable mortgages ||
Fixed mortgage (closed or open)	Variable mortgage (closed or open)
+Payment and interest stay fixed and will never change for the term of the mortgage +The outstanding balance of the mortgage at maturity is known in advance -Interest is usually higher than interest rate on a variable mortgage with the same term -The penalty when you pay off or transfer the mortgage is not known; it can be the interest differential or 3 months of interest, whichever is greater	-Interest might change during the term of the mortgage; it changes with the prime rate -Payments can change if the prime rate rises too much (usually they do not change but stay the same for the whole term) -A mortgage's outstanding balance at maturity is not known in advance; it depends on fluctuations of the prime rate +The penalty when you pay off or transfer the mortgage is usually 3 months of interest +Variable closed mortgage usually can be switched without any penalty to a longer term closed fixed mortgage

You can pay off an open mortgage, sell the property, or contribute a lump sum at any time without any penalty.

On the other hand, **a closed mortgage cannot be prepaid**. If you pay more than a particular allowed amount, sell the property, or pay the mortgage off, you will be penalized (contact your lender to determine the penalty amount).

If you sell your property and buy another one within a very short period of time (typically 90 days, but it depends on the lender), your lender might allow you to transfer your old mortgage to the new property. This way you might avoid penalty, and the only cost to you will usually be legal costs (several hundred dollars).

TIP 31
Locking in rates

Your mortgage lenders can lock rates only 10–15 days prior to the renewal of your mortgage.

If you have a mortgage and it is 120 days (or 90 days) prior to maturity, you cannot lock your rate with the current mortgage lender.

However, you can go to another lender and ask them to guarantee the rate, claiming you want to transfer the mortgage to them (this rate guarantee is free of charge and there is no obligation on your part).

They can guarantee your mortgage rates up to 120 days (although sometimes only 60 or 90 depending on the lender).

This way, if the rate for the renewed mortgage with the current lender does not go down at the maturity date, you can transfer your mortgage to another lender that you locked the rate with.

If you think you are going to sell your property soon, take an open mortgage. If you think you will sell the property in 1 or 2 years, take a closed mortgage for 1 or 2 years; you will save on interest because closed mortgages are less expensive than open ones, everything else being equal.

When you take a mortgage, you have an amortization period (the period of time you need to pay off your mortgage) and a term (the period of time you lock your rate for).

The longer the amortization period, the lower the monthly payment and the longer the period of time for you to pay your interest.

Typically, you have more than one term during the amortization period. It is up to you which term to choose (e.g. 6 months or 3 years) and what type of mortgage to choose (variable or fixed, closed or open).

When the mortgage is up for renewal after the term is over, you can choose another or the same type of mortgage that you want to renew it with.

If you do not decide how to renew it by the maturity day, it is usually renewed for 6 months with an open mortgage which you can change or renew at any time later on. Lenders choose an open mortgage, since they do not want to be sued in case you have to pay a penalty.

Usually, if you have a closed mortgage (fixed or variable), you can renew it with another closed mortgage 90 or 120 days prior to its maturity (depends on the mortgage lender).

When renewing, you can choose any closed mortgage you want (fixed or variable) with any term. Of course, it makes sense to go for an early renewal if the rate is less than it was before.

Lenders allow renewing mortgages 90–120 days prior to maturity because they do not want you to look for better rates with other lenders. If you have a closed mortgage and you want to renew it with an open one without paying a penalty, you have to wait till the maturity date.

Example:

You have a mortgage that is up for renewal in 120 days and your current interest is 4%. You want to early renew, but it does not make sense because the current interest you can renew for is 4.5%.

You cannot lock 4.5% with your current mortgage lender to make sure it does not rise, but you can go to another mortgage provider and lock it with them. If the rate falls to 4.3% when the mortgage is up for renewal, you will renew it with your current mortgage provider; if the rate rises to 4.7%, you will transfer your mortgage to the lender where you locked the rate at 4.5%.

If you have an open mortgage (either fixed or variable), you can renew or pay it off at any time without any penalty.

To renew your mortgage with the same financial institution, you do not need to qualify (lenders do not care if you are employed, unemployed, still have the same marital status, etc.), you just need to choose the new term or interest or mortgage type and sign the renewal agreement.

For the same term, **fixed rates are usually higher than variable rates**. Interest on a fixed rate mortgage will not change during the term of the mortgage. Regardless of what happens to the economy, your rate and the payment will stay the same for the whole term. You know in advance what the outstanding balance of the mortgage will be when you renew your mortgage at maturity.

Variable rates depend on the prime rate. After you sign a variable mortgage, your payment does not usually change if the prime rate goes up or down, but your amortization might go up or down respectively. When the prime rate goes up, the interest you owe

TIP 32
Renew sooner to save

If your lender offers to renew your mortgage 120 days prior to maturity (with a lower rate than the one you currently have), but another lender offers an even better rate when it matures, calculate if it makes more sense to wait and transfer in 120 days or renew it now with the existing lender. In certain cases, you may save more money during these 120 days if you renew immediately with the current lender than if you wait and continue to pay the higher rate until maturity, even though the following rate with the new lender would be the lowest.

TIP 33
Increase your payment to pay it off faster

Consider increasing your mortgage payment by 2–3% every year (to pay it off faster).
However, as mentioned previously, it may be a better idea to maximize your RRSP or RESP contributions instead.

is added to the outstanding balance, so when you renew your mortgage, the balance will be higher and it will take longer to repay it.

In some rare cases if interest goes up too fast (and your interest becomes higher than the payment of your mortgage), your bank might ask you to increase your payments and you will have to comply.

Variable rate mortgages are very good when the prime rate is supposed to go down or stay the same for a long period of time. Fixed rate mortgages are very good when the prime rate is expected to go higher.

The main advantage of a fixed mortgage is that you know in advance how much you pay per period and how much you will owe at maturity. Its main disadvantage is that you will probably pay higher interest or payments than on a similar variable rate mortgage (based on the history).

You can normally switch from a variable closed to a fixed closed mortgage at any time without any penalty, but the mortgage you switch to must be for the same term or longer than the one that you currently have.

Example: Variable closed mortgage

If you have a variable closed mortgage up for renewal in 3 years and 2 months and you want to switch to a fixed closed mortgage, you have to choose a mortgage with the term of 4 years or longer (there is no such term as 3 years and 2 months).

When you start looking for a house, most banks and brokers will lock your interest for 90 or 120 days (this period depends on the lender) when they pre-approve you.

Ask your bank or broker if they can assure you that when they run your credit history for a pre-approval, it does not affect or reduce your credit score (it might be difficult to find such a bank or broker since most mortgage specialists cannot answer this question).

Some lenders lock rates for a specific type of mortgage (e.g. 5-year fixed closed but not 3-year fixed closed), which means that you may have to choose your mortgage type or term before you find a house.

Look for a bank or broker who can lock all available types of mortgages to have more flexibility.

If you lock your interest for 90 to 120 days and mortgage interest rates go down, you will get the lowest rate for the same mortgage type.

Before you apply for a mortgage pre-approval, ask your bank or broker if they will show your credit history to you when they run it. Some banks and brokers do not disclose credit history to the clients claiming it is their (the bank's) property.

If they do not show it to you, you might not qualify without knowing why. Insist on seeing it.

Rent vs. mortgage

It would be wrong to assume that money paid for rent is money that you waste as compared to money paid when you have a mortgage. It is not correct to compare rent payments to mortgage payments this way.

When you have a mortgage you waste a lot of money, too, without thinking about it. In reality, only about 70% (if not less) of your monthly payments for your house go towards paying off your mortgage (i.e. the principal and the interest). The other 30% (or more) is wasted on property taxes, home insurance, property maintenance, utilities, garbage collection, condo fees (if applicable), and many other expenses you have to pay that you do not have when renting (although the rent might sometimes exclude utilities, the rest are most likely included).

Also when you buy or sell a property, you probably pay appraisal and inspection fees, CMHC fees, legal fees, realtor's fees, land transfer tax, GST, and moving expenses.

TIP 34
Co-signing offspring mortgages

When you own a house and your child wants to buy a house but does not qualify for a mortgage on his or her own, you will normally co-sign with them. Make sure that you keep all the records of what you do. When your child sells his or her property, the CRA can audit you and you might pay taxes on the gain (if any) because it is not your primary residence. You will have to prove to CRA that the only intention to add you on the mortgage was to buy the property for your child (obviously, it has to be his or her primary residence when they sell the property; otherwise CRA will not accept your claim).
Make sure that you do not pay for the property but that your child does. Speak with an accountant before helping your child to buy a house.

TIP 35
Mortgage insurance

If you consider transferring your mortgage from one financial institution to another and you have life or disability insurance on your mortgage, make sure that you get comparable insurance with the other lender. You might be non-insurable or the new insurance cost might offset all the benefits of transferring your mortgage.

Any fixing that needs to be done in your house is paid out of your pocket when you have a mortgage, while such expenses are normally fully covered by your landlord if you rent.

There are some other disadvantages of having your own house, as the interest rate of the mortgage and/or property taxes and/or property insurance can go higher, which you cannot negotiate. While rent can increase, too, it is normally negotiable with your landlord. You cannot stop mortgage payments right away, as you typically have to sell the property first (or pay some kind of (substantial) penalty for breaking the mortgage), while you can usually stop rent payments and move out with just a reasonable notice.

Moreover, the value of the property can go down (which will affect you as a house owner but will not have any effect on you if you rent); you might have to pay legal fees and taxes when you buy (and legal fees when you sell, in some provinces); you have to put a substantial amount of down payment when you buy a house (and you have to pay CMHC fees if your down payment is less than 20%), while you do not have these issues when renting. (See rates at the CMHC site at http://artemfinancial.ca/links/cmhc-fees.)

Some people would agree with this analysis but would also argue that much of each monthly payment still goes towards their home equity. While this is true, it will still be a problem if the value of the house drops 20% and your home equity disappears. Do not assume it cannot happen. When you want to stop renting and consider buying a house instead, take all these factors into consideration.

When you sell your primary residence you do not pay income tax on the gain (which is the appreciation between the price you initially paid and the price you sold your property for). Refer to http://artemfinancial.ca/links/principal-residence to find out what is considered your primary residence.

Although you might have been paying for your house for a long period of time, remember that you may still lose, even if you have a very small mortgage which you fail to pay off.

An RRSP (and even an RESP) provides you with extra savings you can benefit from immediately, and in case of an emergency, you can use those savings to pay other expenses (however you cannot extract bricks from your house and sell them if you need money).

Your house is not your savings or a retirement plan, it is simply another consumer goods category which is not much different from your car or computer. Even if it appreciates in value, you still need to have liquid savings.

Bank vs. mortgage broker and how to choose

One is not better or worse than the other, as long as they provide you with good service. The financial institution is less important in most cases. What really matters is the professional you are going to work with (and his or her credentials and designations).

Ask how long the person has been in the business. Do they have a mortgage? If you have questions after your mortgage is signed, will this individual help you?

If you do not have a good credit history, mortgage brokers can still often find a lender who will lend you money.

Do not look for the lowest rate. The lowest rate is the lowest for a reason; mortgages are a very competitive business. The rate is very important, but if someone gives you a mortgage with 0% and you have to pay penalties and fines for his or her mistakes in the future, it is probably not the best deal.

When you look for a mortgage professional, make sure that you make an application with a person you want to deal with in the future because many banks do not want you to switch from one person to another, and many mortgage specialists will be reluctant to work with you if you started with someone else at the same financial institution.

**TIP 36
Ask for a property tax reassessment**

Your property tax depends on the value of your house. If you think that the value of your house is lower than the City claims it to be (see City Assessment statement), you can ask the City to reassess the value, and you will pay less property tax if the reassessment confirms that the value is indeed lower. Keep in mind that it is in the City's best interest to keep the value of your property higher, not lower.
The reassessment normally costs a small non-refundable fee.

TIP 37
Transferring your mortgage

If you want to transfer your mortgage to another mortgage lender and you have to pay penalty due to breaking the mortgage contract, prepay 10% (or any allowed amount) of the mortgage. This will reduce the penalty because the penalty is calculated based on the (current) outstanding mortgage balance.

Even if you need to borrow money to prepay the mortgage, it's most likely that you'll save on the penalty more than what you'll pay for the interest on the borrowed money. Please keep in mind that some FIs calculate the penalty assuming you already paid allowed prepayment. Check with your FI if this is the case.

Questions to ask:

1. Does the mortgage professional do "pre-approval" or just a "rate hold" (another name is "rate guarantee")? Pre-approvals are generally seen as being more thorough and underwritten while a rate hold is simply a rate guarantee. If it is just a rate hold, you might not actually qualify for a mortgage in the future when you find a property you want to buy.

2. How is the mortgage professional compensated?

3. Is it a collateral or a conventional mortgage? It is a good idea to ask for a guarantee that it will be registered as a conventional mortgage (in case you are interested in one).

4. Can you pay a lump sum without a penalty (and if there is a penalty, what is it)?

5. Can you increase regular mortgage payments (e.g. double up payments), and if you can, then by how much?

6. Can you sell or pay off the mortgage (some lenders do not allow that, even with a penalty)?

7. Can you renew your mortgage early (within 120 days prior to maturity) without a penalty?

8. What is the cost of the life or disability mortgage insurance, and how much is the discount if you apply jointly with someone and both of you take insurance types?

9. Will your spouse qualify for a disability insurance, assuming you want a disability insurance and your spouse does not work?

10. Can you switch your mortgage to another property if you sell the existing one?

Always compare rates with similar mortgage options; do not compare just rates on offered mortgages.

When you are pre-approved for a mortgage, ask your mortgage professional if the (biweekly or monthly) payment quote is final. In many cases, lenders do not disclose certain commission costs, legal fees, and other extra charges that are not related to the mortgage itself, and when you close the deal you may get nasty surprises.

When you have a mortgage and you need to borrow money (for any purpose), you can take a second mortgage or a line of credit against your property (both are referred to as "second mortgage" because it is registered on title as a second mortgage).

You must have equity in your house (i.e. the first mortgage plus the second mortgage combined should be substantially lower than the total value of the property). The percentage of equity you have to own depends on specific regulations, and you should ask your lender.

There are two ways to borrow money against your property:

1. Some lenders can register a bigger amount to be your first and the only mortgage registered on title and then they split the amount between your initial mortgage and the new mortgage or line of credit.

    Example: Larger mortgage

    The value of your house is $300,000 and your initial mortgage is $75,000. You want to have a $25,000 line of credit. The lender can register $100,000 as your first and only mortgage registered on title but then split it between a $75,000 mortgage and a $25,000 line of credit.

2. You can get a second mortgage and it will be second on your title. This means that if you do not pay your mortgage and your house is sold, the lender with the first mortgage on title gets money first, and then the second lender gets the remainder.

Mortgages that are second on title usually have a higher interest rate because the risk for the lender is higher. These two mortgages can be given by the same or by different lenders.

TIP 38
Title fraud

It is very important to be aware of title frauds. Title frauds happen when someone steals your identity and uses it either to sell your house or to take a first or second mortgage on the property and uses the money. You remain unaware until the lender starts calling you about late mortgage payments or strangers appear and want to know what you are doing in their house. People have lost their homes because of this, and the laws regulating who is responsible for losses may vary.

A title fraud may happen to a person with or without a mortgage registered on a title (meaning the mortgage was paid off a long time ago). However, homeowners without a mortgage are at an increased risk for this type of fraud. This is because a lawyer is involved when a home with a mortgage is sold, and a lawyer may notice a fraud. Seniors are particularly at risk since impostors will think that seniors are less knowledgeable about identity theft and will choose them as targets more often.

Even if you do not need a mortgage or line of credit, it might be a good idea to ask your bank to register a line of credit on the title. Another way to protect yourself from title frauds is to buy title insurance.

If you need to borrow extra money against your property (pull out equity), you will have to qualify first based on your income, credit history, etc. In most cases, your lender will request an appraisal of the property. Often it is you who pays for the appraisal and registration of the new mortgage on title (regardless of whether it is registered as first or second, see above).

Make sure that you know all of the costs before you get your second mortgage because appraisals and registrations are not cheap.

You can have life and disability insurance on a mortgage (see explanation about that in the insurance section).

Chapter 6 notes

Please use this space for your notes.

Chapter 7: POWER OF ATTORNEY, ENDURING POWER OF ATTORNEY, AND WILLS

TIP 39
Present your POA to your bank

Even if you are a healthy individual and do not anticipate being ill soon, present your POA (but not EPOA) to your bank and ask them to make notes on your profile. Notify your attorney that your bank has a record about the POA.

In case something happens, your attorney does not need to run to your bank and ask them to approve your POA. Such a request will be delayed, and the bank might decline the POA because the attorney, rather than you, presents the POA.

A power of attorney (POA) means you (the donor) designate someone (the attorney) to act on your behalf. You can do a general POA at your bank and/or with a lawyer. A general POA done at the bank is valid only for the specific bank it is done at. You can request to cancel a POA at any time. If you do a POA with a lawyer it will be good for any service, not just for your bank.

Make sure that you designate someone who you fully trust, since banks will not be liable if your attorney withdraws your money and spends it. The attorney can make decisions about your property or financial affairs. This means that they can operate your bank accounts, pay your bills, and sell or buy property or shares on your behalf.

There are certain things the attorney cannot do. For example, they cannot change your investment profile (e.g. from low risk to high risk), they cannot add or change beneficiaries or add themselves to your account for it to become joint (but the attorney still has full access to the account if the POA/EPOA indicates that).

An enduring power of attorney (EPOA) is a power of attorney that is only intended to be brought into force if the donor becomes or is becoming mentally incapable. This type of power of attorney cannot be done at the bank.

The difference between POA and EPOA is that a general power of attorney stops being in effect after the donor loses the mental capacity to make financial decisions, but an EPOA will continue to have effect even after the donor loses mental capacity.

It is worth mentioning an additional POA for personal care that gives your designated attorney the power to make decisions on your behalf in relation to medical issues, hospitalization, and long-term care when you are no longer capable of making such decisions yourself. A doctor will decide if you are able to make such decisions.

A will goes into effect on the day you die. A POA/EPOA applies while you are alive and ceases to apply when you die. You need both a POA/EPOA and a will, as they complement each other and do not overlap.

A will is probably the best way to ensure your estate is managed based on your decisions.

Basic will templates are available online (often free of charge), but you still need to customize them and make sure that they are valid and legal. Consider time and effort spent on this against the fee you will pay to a professional lawyer (notary in Quebec) to write your own will from scratch.

There is a difference between common-law and legal spouse. For example, unlike legal spouses, common-law spouses do not have automatic entitlement to the assets of their common-law spouse after his or her death, even if there is a will.

Do not designate a person to be your executor just because they are your relative or friend. Dealing with estate affairs is an extremely complicated issue, and your executor has to have some financial skills and be very organized.

Designating a proper paid executor (who can be a person unrelated to you or even a financial company) is a good idea, especially if you have several beneficiaries and substantial assets.

Try to avoid designating several executors because every simple task will have to be done by all of them (meaning all of them will have to sign letters of direction, receipts, and so on).

TIP 40
Don't delay – get a POA/EPOA/will

Drafting a POA/EPOA/will is inexpensive when compared to the expense potentially created by not having one in place when the need arises. Cost should not be a reason for you to postpone the process of creating your POA/EPOA/will.

TIP 41
No beneficiary as executor

If you want to designate several beneficiaries for your estate, do not designate one of your beneficiaries to be an executor of the estate. This will avoid a conflict of interest.

When you designate an executor, always make sure that they will be paid for the work. Also, keep in mind that a good friend of yours will not necessarily be a good executor, as this job requires specific knowledge and skills. There are estate companies (trust and estate services) that can help to delegate executors' duties.

TIP 42
List your important information for your executor

Make a list of personal assets, liabilities, credit cards, account numbers, and other things your executor (liquidator in Quebec) will need to deal with. Make sure that the person you designate as an executor of your estate knows that they are the executor and are aware of the list and its location.

In your will, you can designate a successor executor who assumes the position if the prior designated executor fails to qualify or ceases to act.

If you keep your will at a safe deposit box at your bank, let your executor know where it is and provide the key to the box.

Dealing with an estate is an extremely complicated issue. In this situation, we can only base our decisions on records and directions left by the deceased person, and cannot ask them questions. If you wish to minimize your estate tax and want your beneficiaries to receive what YOU and not the government or court want them to receive, find a qualified estate planner.

Planning your estate is a lengthy process, so allow enough time instead of waiting until the last minute. There is no way back to fix or redo certain things after the person passes away. Things that sound rational to you are not necessarily rational to the court when beneficiaries try to sue each other for receiving different assets or amounts of money.

Chapter 7 notes

Please use this space for your notes.

Chapter 8: INSURANCE

You have several insurance options to choose from:

1. no insurance whatsoever

2. credit insurance

3. personal insurance (or insurance at work)

4. a combination of 2 and 3

In general, having protection is a good thing, so I will only discuss options 2 through 4.

Credit insurance

Credit insurance is insurance that is attached to a credit product (e.g. line of credit, mortgage, etc.). You get it only when you apply or qualify for credit from your bank (lender). This insurance does not exist independently without a credit product.

There are normally two credit insurance types which you have to qualify for: life and disability protections (as many banks like to call insurance types). When there is an outstanding balance (debt), insurance charges you premiums along with your debt payments. When you do not owe anything, you pay nothing for either insurance. Some banks allow you to have "life insurance only," "life and disability," or "disability only," but some lenders do not allow disability insurance on its own without life insurance.

It is your responsibility to notify the insurance provider about your medical issues before you accept this kind of insurance. Insurance companies will waive the coverage, and you will get only your premiums back if you do not notify them about medical conditions before you accept the coverage. If your medical issues arise after you took your insurance, you remain covered.

The insurance cost usually depends on the credit product and your age. Premiums are about the same from one financial institution to the other.

If you have a co-signer, you will need to choose who will be covered. Life insurance costs significantly less than disability insurance because one can die only once, while it is possible to become disabled many times throughout one's life.

Disability insurance covers permanent disability and temporary disabilities which prevent you from working. Insurance companies usually start paying disability insurance after a 90-day waiting period, so if the time when you cannot work is less than 90 days, this period will not be covered.

Here is a **big difference between a personal insurance and a credit insurance** that might surprise many people:

- You are not the beneficiary of the credit insurance.
- Your money lender is the beneficiary.
- This means that you will not receive any proceeds, and in case of disability, your debt balance might not diminish by much when you recover and go back to work.

Things are different for personal life or disability insurance:

- The beneficiary of personal insurance (in the case of disability insurance, you are the beneficiary of your own insurance) receives the money and decides what they want to spend it on.

Credit disability insurance usually covers minimum monthly payments of your credit product up to 2 years or till you can work again, whichever happens earlier.

Credit life insurance is paid when the insured person passes away. Your spouse, children, or any other relatives will not receive any insurance proceeds; the insurance will pay off the outstanding balance of the debt you have insurance on.

Underwriting on a typical mortgage insurance claim is done after the fact. In other words, the insurance company will look into the medical history of the deceased to see if there could be any reasons for denying the claim, to begin with.

For personal insurance, underwriting is done beforehand. Therefore, an insurance claim cannot be denied later on (unless there is a fraud involved).

Another big surprise to many people is that **credit insurance premiums can change over time** (and they usually go up). Changes do not happen often, but the premiums are not guaranteed and subject to change.

If you have personal insurance, your premiums are constant and do not change (although some types of insurance can change)

Balance protector insurance (insurance for your credit card)

This insurance is designed to cover your monthly minimum credit card payments in case of loss of income due to job loss or extreme illness, or pay your balance in the event of death. If you have several credit cards, you can have coverage on each one. This insurance is very expensive.

Personal insurance

Only insurance companies can issue personal insurance. Since insurance is not related to banking per se, this topic is only briefly covered in this book.

The subject of personal insurance is very broad and companies have different products.

If you are an employee, you might have long- and short-term disability insurance from work. You are the beneficiary of your disability insurance.

A long-term disability insurance usually covers up to 66–70% of your gross income. A short-term disability insurance might cover 100% of your income, but as per its name, it is only good for several months.

A long-term disability insurance ceases payments at age 65 of the recipient (which is the age of receiving Canada or Quebec Pension).

In case the insured person gets ill with underlying disability, he or she will receive a monthly income.

This will not be taxable if the insured person paid policy premiums himself or herself. If premiums were paid by the employer (and the employee or the insured person never paid taxes on the premiums), then it will be taxable.

There are some other types of "disability" insurance that you might consider (your employer might offer them to you as well). You can have these types of insurance regardless of your income and employment status.

These types of insurance are especially important for self-employed or unemployed people, as mentioned before.

- **Critical Illness insurance**. If the insured person is diagnosed with an underlying illness (life threatening illnesses such as cancer, heart attacks, strokes, etc.) they will receive a tax-free lump sum.

- **Long-Term Care insurance**. This insurance is paid monthly when the insured person is unable to care for themselves due to a chronic illness or cognitive impairment. The conditions for receiving this insurance are much stricter than for regular disability insurance. Some of the important advantages comparing this to disability insurance are: the person is covered till death instead of age 65, it is cheaper, and you can choose your own coverage (i.e. it is not limited to 66–70% of individual's income).

Life insurance is paid to your estate or any beneficiary(ies) that you designate. The beneficiary(ies) decides what to do with the life insurance proceeds.

The beneficiary gets life insurance proceeds tax free. If the insurance premiums were paid by the employing company, then you must pay tax on them. You can have several life insurance policies (e.g. one at work and a personal life insurance you purchased on you own). Life insurance proceeds can sometimes be paid to the owner of the insurance if they can provide a proof (e.g. a written confirmation from their physician outlining the diagnosis) confirming that their life expectancy is less than 12 or 24 months.

There are two types of life insurance: term and permanent (a permanent insurance can also be referred to as "Universal Life Insurance," "Whole Life Insurance," or "Term 100 Life Insurance"). Term insurance is issued for a certain period of time, e.g. 10 or 20 years. If the person is alive after this period, his or her beneficiaries receive nothing.

In many cases, term insurance can be renewed with increased premiums. Permanent insurance is for life and will kick in when the person passes away, no matter when it happens.

Do not assume that bigger insurance coverage costs more than smaller coverage amounts. $200,000 of coverage can be more expensive than $250,000 because your insurance company may re-insure itself with another company, and you will pay smaller premiums because of that.

Term 100 life insurance is the simplest to understand, and it is sometimes the cheapest permanent life insurance available. It provides coverage for as long as you live, regardless of when you pass away; your premiums never change; and if you are alive at age 100, your premiums (but not the coverage) cease.

Another type of permanent insurance is "Universal Life" insurance. This type of insurance has two parts: the life insurance and the investment portion (called "cash value of the policy").

You have to pay premiums to have just the life insurance, but you can optionally also pay more, up to a certain amount, which goes to the investment portion. The investment portion is invested in different mutual funds (which you or your investment advisor choose), and when you die, your beneficiary gets both the life insurance and the investment portion tax free.

Whole Life and Universal Life policies might have "cash surrender value," which will be paid to you (minus applicable fees) in case you terminate the policy. Cash surrender value can be used in case of emergency or can be assigned as collateral for a loan.

Tips to save money on your personal and car insurance

1. The smaller your deductible, the higher your insurance cost premium. If you increase the deductible to $500 or even $1,000, it will decrease your premiums significantly. The logic is simple: you should protect yourself from high losses, not small ones. In many cases if the damage is less than $1,000, you probably will not contact your insurance company anyway because your claim might increase your premiums in the future.

2. If you bundle several insurance policies (e.g. car and home or two car insurance policies) with the same insurance company, you will usually get a discount.

3. Look for an insurance broker who has access to many insurance companies. Brokers can get you a better deal from the insurance company than you can get contacting the company directly.

4. Some insurance companies charge a certain category of drivers (e.g. males younger than 25 years old) higher premiums because they have bad experience with this category of drivers. Compare prices across different companies and ask why their premiums are higher or lower than those of their competitors.

5. Some companies give you a discount if you get an insurance quote online.

6. Check if your employer has negotiated a group discount with an insurance provider.

7. If you are a member of a professional group or alumni association, you may qualify for special rates with a particular insurer.

8. Stay away from insurance companies that offer significantly lower premiums (20%) than their competitors.

9. If your insurance did not cover some of your medical expenses or you did not claim the expenses, consider combining the claim for expenses incurred by you, your spouse or partner, and your eligible dependents for any 12-month period ending in the current year, to optimize your tax savings. The federal government provides a non-refundable credit of 15% on eligible medical expenses (up to a certain limit) that add up to more than 3% of your net income (in Quebec, the threshold is 3% of the net family income).

You can find brochures about car, home, and business insurance at the IBC site accessible at http://artemfinancial.ca/links/insurance-brochures.

Chapter 8 notes

Please use this space for your notes.

Chapter 9: REGISTERED PROGRAMS

These are the most common registered savings programs:

- RRSP/LIRA/Group RRSP

- Spousal RRSP

- RRIF and LIF

- RESP

- TFSA

Pension options (for employed people only):

- defined benefit plans

- defined contribution plans

RRSPs and LIRAs are programs to save money for your retirement. This chapter discusses RRSPs.

There are many types of LIRA programs, including LRSP, LIRA (provincial jurisdiction), and locked-in RRSP (federal jurisdiction). They are all similar and are referred to as LIRA in this book hereafter.

Two major differences between an RRSP and a LIRA are that only your employer contributes to LIRA, and you cannot withdraw funds from a LIRA until it is converted to LIF (see below).

How RRSPs work

An RRSP reduces your taxable income by the amount you contribute to the RRSP (not every type of income is eligible for the RRSP contribution limit. Eligible income is employment earnings (i.e. salary), rental income, alimony received, net business income, and disability benefits paid by the Canada Pension Plan or Québec Pension Plan).

Example: RRSP

Say you are an employee or are self-employed and you make $50,000 per year before taxes (for a self-employed person, $50,000 after expenses but before taxes). You worked in 2013, and you have created RRSP room for 2014.

Amount that you are allowed to contribute to RRSP (http://artemfinancial.ca/links/max-rrsp) in 2014 is 18% of your 2013 income plus whatever RRSP room you created in previous years. If in 2014 you decide to contribute $5,000 into an RRSP, your taxable income in 2014 is now $45,000 rather than $50,000.

When you file your 2014 income tax in March 2015, you are going to get a tax refund for what you overpaid in taxes. If you do not contribute the maximum allowed to your RRSP in that year, you can carry the unused portion forward indefinitely. You can contribute 18% of your previous year's income up to a certain maximum amount (which changes every year), but you will get a refund next year. When you file your income tax return, you receive your Notice of Assessment showing your income and the RRSP room that you have.

To summarize, you contribute to an RRSP today (e.g. 2014) based on your previous year(s) of income (2013 and previous years), and you get a refund next year (2015).

You can over-contribute to your RRSP up to $2,000 per lifetime, but you do not get any deductions on such over-contribution.

You might not get any refund if you contribute to an RRSP through your work during the year and your employer deducts less tax from you as these contributions are taken into account (i.e. your tax would be higher without them).

You do not need to be a permanent resident of Canada to contribute to an RRSP (since your room is created by your income), but you have to work in Canada legally to qualify.

If you are a member of a defined benefit or contribution pension (see explanation about DB/DC below), you may transfer it to a LIRA when you leave your employer.

Distributions of income from master limited partnerships (MLPs) are generally distributions of business income, which are treated differently from dividends paid on U.S. stocks. As a result, MLP income in Canada is subject to a withholding tax, which is <u>not</u> reduced according to the Canada-U.S. tax treaty. There is no way to avoid this tax if you hold these types of investments in your RRSP.

If MLPs or foreign non-U.S. stocks are held in a non-registered account, you may be entitled to a foreign tax credit for some of the withholding tax against Canadian tax payable on that investment income.

Consult your tax advisor before purchasing MLPs and/or foreign stocks.

RRSP withdrawals

You can withdraw money from an RRSP at any time using any (or a combination) of the three options below.

1. You can withdraw money from an RRSP directly (and pay a withholding tax at the time of your withdrawal).

2. You can convert your RRSP to an RRIF and withdraw at least the minimum amount from the RRIF every year (the RRIF program is explained below).

3. You can buy an annuity (also explained below); every amount received is taxed.

RRSP Withdrawals

Direct withdrawals
• Other direct withdrawals: a withholding tax is paid upon withdrawal.
• To buy a home or to pay for education; no taxes if the money is returned to the RRSP within a period of time.
Conversion to RRIF
• Withdraw the annual minimum amount: a tax is paid next year.
• Withdraw more than the annual minimum amount: a tax for the minimum amount is paid next year; a withholding tax for the difference is paid upon withdrawal.
Annuity purchase
• Every amount received is taxed.

There are two exceptions when you can withdraw money directly from an RRSP and not pay income tax (please use the provided links to review the complete set of rules applying to each exception):

- **Home Buyers' Plan (HBP)**: if you buy a house and neither you nor your spouse or common-law spouse owned a house in the last 5 years. The maximum each spouse can withdraw is $25,000 (as of 2014). You have to put it back into RRSP within 15 years. The repayment period begins the second year after the year you withdrew money from RRSP, and you have to repay at least 1/15 of the total amount you withdrew in each year of your repayment period. Please visit http://artemfinancial.ca/links/hbp for more information.

- **Lifelong Learning Plan**: if you or your spouse go to school and need to pay for education. As of 2014, the maximum each spouse can withdraw is $20,000 (not exceeding $10,000 annually).You have to put it back in RRSP within 10 years (you have to repay at least 1/10 of the total amount you withdrew in each year of your repayment period). Please visit http://artemfinancial.ca/links/llp for more information.

If you do not return the money to your RRSP within the set time frame, it will be added to your income for that year, and you will be taxed based on your tax bracket. You do not need to return money to the same RRSP account or the same financial institution it was taken from.

You do not pay any tax on the income you have in an RRSP until you withdraw money from it (regardless if it is interest, dividend, or capital gain).

When you withdraw money directly from an RRSP, you have to pay a withholding tax (regardless of your age). It is not a penalty or extra tax; CRA simply wants to get their share before you file your income tax for that year.

There are some exceptions when you can ask CRA not to withdraw tax, but you have to receive an approval letter from CRA to avoid paying this withholding tax at the time of withdrawal.

The withholding tax is 10%, 20%, or 30%, depending on a withdrawn amount per year and not per transaction (i.e. it is not legal to withdraw, let's say, $5,000 three times to save on tax to get $15,000 in total; refer to the table below). Please note that Quebec residents will have a different tax.

All provinces except Quebec

Withdrawn amount	Withholding tax
Up to $5,000	10%
$5,000.01 to $15,000	20%
$15,000.01 and over	30%

Quebec residents only (combined with Federal tax)

Withdrawn amount	Withholding tax
Up to $5,000	21%
$5,000.01 to $15,000	26%
$15,000.01 and over	31%

Since withdrawals from RRSPs are not different from your employment income, when you file your income tax for that year, the RRSP withdrawal amount should be added to all other sources of income. If you overpaid tax on the total income, you will get a refund; if you underpaid, you will have to pay what you still owe.

There is no maximum or minimum for withdrawals from RRSPs. You can withdraw any amount and as many times as you wish.

Note: Please note that you might not be able to withdraw from your RRSP if you have, for example, a non-redeemable GIC. In this case, the withdrawal restriction is due to the investment you have in the RRSP and not due to the RRSP itself.

It makes sense to contribute to your RRSP when your current total taxable income is higher than your anticipated total income when you retire (e.g. current $100,000 salary vs. $40,000 income when you retire).

It does not make sense to contribute to an RRSP when the opposite happens (e.g. current salary is $20,000 but retirement income is $65,000). It does not make sense to receive a refund which will be smaller than what you will pay in income tax in the future. There are many reasons why the retirement income can be higher than your current income. For example, pension or RRIF might be transferred from the deceased spouse.

The only exception to this rule (whether you contribute to an RRSP or not) is when you have a group RRSP at work and your employer matches your RRSP contribution (for example, when you contribute 5% and your employer contributes 5% as well).

In this case you get free money, and it does make sense to contribute to the RRSP regardless of your current and future tax bracket(s). Please note, group RRSPs do not mean that your employer would contribute money if you do, but sometimes it is just an option for all employees of a certain company to contribute to an RRSP.

Chapter 9 notes

Please use this space for your notes.

Chapter 10: RESP & TFSA

RESP

The RESP is a tax-sheltered education savings account that was created to help you save for the education of (primarily) your children and grandchildren (however, you can in principle contribute to any person's RESP).

To read about RESP in different languages, please visit http://artemfinancial.ca/links/resp.

There are three types of RESP: individual, family and group.

Group (multiple beneficiaries) RESP

A group RESP accommodates contributions of multiple families who buy plan units. The time of enrolment is set in advance, based on the child's birth date, and this is when the plan matures. At this point, all children of the same age will share and use the accumulated earnings. If your child does not begin post-secondary studies at that time, the earnings you receive from the plan might be affected. Moreover, if you drop out of the plan before it matures, you will lose all your earnings. This is the least popular option.

Individual (single beneficiary) and Family (multiple beneficiaries) RESP

Anyone can open an individual RESP and contribute to it. This includes parents, grandparents, aunts, uncles, and friends. You can also contribute to an individual plan for yourself.

A family RESP can have one or more beneficiaries, but each beneficiary must be related to the contributor by blood or adoption ("related by blood" includes child or grandchild or brother or sister but not nephew or niece).

The beneficiaries must be under 21 when they are named. Contributions can only be made until at least one beneficiary is under 21 years old and at least one has to pursue post-secondary education to get government grants and earnings. It is up to you to decide how to split the money between the beneficiaries.

This RESP plan is the most popular and is offered by most financial institutions.

To make the explanation simple, let's say that the individual or family plan has three parts:

1. **Your contributions**: You can contribute up to $50,000 per lifetime of the plan to each beneficiary. Your contributions are not tax deductible. When your contributions are withdrawn from the RESP, no tax will be paid.

2. **Government grants**: The federal government will provide a grant (a Canada Education Savings Grant) of 20% of your first $2,500 in annual contributions per beneficiary (i.e. up to $500 per beneficiary). You might receive more than 20% if your family, not individual, income is low. It does not matter if you pay a lump sum or make periodic contributions over the course of the same year.

   If you did not contribute or contributed less than $2,500 one year, you can catch up in the following years, but then the maximum annual grant from the federal government is $1,000 (corresponding to at least $5,000 of your contribution). The maximum lifetime grant per beneficiary that you can receive from the federal government is $7,200.

   Some provinces provide additional grants. If the beneficiary goes to school and withdraws any grant portion from the RESP, they pay tax on it based on their tax bracket.

3. **Growth (of your contributions and grants)**: Depending on how you invest your contributions and grants, you (presumably) will incur some growth of those investments either in the form of interest (e.g. in case you invest them in GICs) or gain (e.g. if you invest them in mutual funds).

You do not pay tax on this growth as long as it stays in the RESP. If the beneficiary goes to school and withdraws some growth portion from the RESP, they will pay tax on it based on their tax bracket.

A Comparison of RESP Providers

	Banks	Mutual Fund Companies	Investment Dealers
Plans provided	Individual and family plans but not group plans		
Typical investment options	-savings accounts -GICs -mutual funds	-mutual funds -GICs (not all FIs offer them)	-T-bills -bonds -mutual funds -stocks
Investment decision	You (or your advisor) choose an appropriate investment.		
Contributions	You decide when and how much to contribute (up to the lifetime limit).		
Fees	-Sales charges and MER if you buy mutual funds -Management fees, which could include trustee fees and administrative fees if you buy mutual funds -Commissions if you buy or sell stocks or bonds There are generally no fees when you buy GICs, Canada Savings Bonds, and other deposit products. There are generally no sales charges if you buy mutual funds from a bank.		
Withdrawals or cancellation of the plan (other than when the beneficiary(ies) start(s) school	You can withdraw your contributions at any time, after paying fees if any. There are no taxes on contribution withdrawals. You may have to return any grants on those contributions to the government. You can withdraw the earnings if you meet certain conditions. If you take the earnings out in cash, you'll have to pay tax. In some cases, you can reduce or eliminate the tax by transferring the earnings to your RRSP.		
Money transfer to another child	Money can be transferred.		
Transfer RESP to another FI	The transfer fee is usually low.		

RESP Providers: Scholarship Plan Dealers

	RESP Provider: Scholarship Plan Dealers
Plans provided	Individual, family, and group plans
Typical investment options	In general, your plan must invest in low(er) risk investments such as T-bills, GICs, and bonds.
Investment decision	All of the investment decisions are made for you. You are not a decision maker.
Contributions	If you have an individual or family plan, you decide when and how much to contribute (up to the lifetime and (sometimes) annual limits). If you have a group plan, contributions are made based on a given schedule. If a scheduled contribution is missed, your plan may be annulled or you may have to pay a penalty.
Fees	-Enrolment fees -Administration fees -Investment management fees -Depository fees -Trustee fees Most fees are deducted from your early contributions; they are not based on performance.
Withdrawals or cancellation of the plan (other than when the beneficiary(ies) start(s) school)	These plans may have more restrictions than other types of plans on how much and how often you can make withdrawals. Different plans have different restrictions. It is very important to check the prospectus before you open a plan.
Money transfer to another child	Money can be transferred in individual and family plans. Money cannot be transferred in a group plan.
Transfer RESP to another FI	The transfer fee can be very high.

Example: Family Plan RESP

The family plan is the most common and popular RESP. It is discussed in more detail below.

Family RESP		
Contribution per child	**Grants per child**	**Growth per child**
Up to $50,000 per lifetime; not tax deductible; no tax upon withdrawal.	Up to $1,000 per year and $7,200 per lifetime from the Federal Government; might qualify for extra Federal grants (based on family income) and grants from the Provincial Government; taxable income to the child who goes to school.	You get income from your contributions and grant investments. The taxable income goes to the child who goes to school, which is a tax savings. The funds can be withdrawn or transferred to an RRSP if the child does not go to school.

A family RESP has to have at least one beneficiary related to the subscriber by blood or adoption (see description above).

There are only two scenarios with the family RESP:

- nobody goes to school

- at least one child goes to school

In the family plan, it does not matter how many children pursue post-secondary education. As long as at least one of the beneficiaries does, they will benefit from the RESP.

Example: Withdrawing from the Family Plan RESP

(RESP contributions can be withdrawn anytime without taxes)			
Going to school		**Not going to school**	
One child	**More than one child**	**RESP exists for 10+ years, the child is 21+ years old**	**RESP exists for less than 10 years or the child is younger than 21 years old**
The child gets all the grants and growth.	You decide how to split grants and growth between children.	Growth withdrawal or transfer to RRSP are possible; grants are returned to the government.	Grants are returned to the government. Growth withdrawal or transfer to RRSP are only possible when the above conditions are met.

If nobody in the family plan pursues post-secondary education:

You can withdraw your contributions at any time without any taxes owed (keep in mind that you might have to pay a penalty to the provider of the RESP for withdrawing money from the RESP). If you collapse (close) your RESP and if certain conditions are met, you can transfer some of the growth to your RRSP. You do not receive grants if none of the children pursue post-secondary education. They will be returned to the government.

If at least one child pursues post-secondary education:

When your child goes to school, you withdraw money from the RESP, and the child pays tax on government grants and the growth, the same as on regular income based on his or her tax bracket. The child does not pay tax on your contributions (you have already paid tax on them before contributing to the RESP).

To use the RESP money, your child(ren) can enrol for post-secondary education in Canada or even outside of Canada. A list of Designated Educational Institutions can be found at http://artemfinancial.ca/links/resp-list-schools.

TFSAs

The Tax-Free Savings Account (TFSA) allows each Canadian resident (http://artemfinancial.ca/links/who-is-resident), aged 18 and over, to set money aside tax-free throughout their lifetime (if the age of majority is 19 years old in your province and you are turning 18 years old, you will accumulate TFSA contribution room for that year, but you cannot open and contribute to a TFSA before you turn 19).

Starting January 1, 2009, you were allowed to contribute up to $5,000 each calendar year, plus any unused TFSA contribution room from the previous year(s) and the amount you withdrew the year(s) before. Starting in 2013, the contribution limit became $5,500 per year instead of $5,000.

The following example will help you understand these regulations better.

Example: TFSA contributions

If you maximized your contribution from 2009 to 2012 (i.e. contributed $20,000) and you withdrew any amount in 2012 (e.g. $500), you will not be able to contribute that amount back the same year (2012). You will have to wait till at least January 2013 and then contribute whatever you withdrew then (e.g. $500) in addition to the maximum of $5,500 for that year (2013).

Note that TFSA withdrawals are tax free. They are not counted as income and are not reported in your income tax filing.

You can (and in fact should) designate a beneficiary on this plan. You can also name a spouse or partner to be the successor annuitant of the TFSA in case you die.

This is similar to the RRIF successor annuitant designation. The successor annuitant can only be the spouse or the partner of the person who owns the TFSA; no one else qualifies. That person will take control of the TFSA when the original account holder passes away.

The successor annuitant will not be able to make new contributions to the plan, but they can make a new beneficiary designation and may cash out the plan at any time, tax free. A beneficiary is a person named to inherit a plan's assets: a relative, friend, or charity. After the beneficiary inherits all the TFSA assets, tax free, the plan is discontinued. Note that any income that accumulates in the TFSA between the holder's death and the date it is terminated is taxable to the beneficiary. If you make a mistake and name your spouse as a beneficiary, the Canada Revenue Agency will probably interpret that as meaning "successor holder."

Chapter 10 notes

Please use this space for your notes.

Chapter 11: FUTURE (RETIREMENT) INCOME

People rarely know what income to expect when they retire.

To find out if you should contribute to RRSPs, you have to know what income you will have at the age of retirement (usually 65 years old). Your total retirement income may consist of:

- your employment income (if you still work) and/or pension plans from work

- investment income (e.g. withdrawals from RRSP or RRIF, income from non-registered investments, rental property income)

- OAS

- CPP or QPP

- GIS or Allowance (which are non-taxable but must be reported while filing income tax returns)

You may also have additional sources of income, such as royalty income, scholarships, etc.

Employment income

On average, employment income reaches its peak between the age of 50 and 60. If you receive a pension from work, it will be taxed at the same rate as your salary.

Investment income

First, you need to calculate the value of your investment based on your present savings plus all contributions you are planning to have over the years. Use the "Compound Interest Calculator" at http://artemfinancial.ca/links/calculators to calculate what your total investment portfolio will be worth. Use 4–5% annual conservative rate of return. You will accumulate wealth not by increasing the risk or return of the investments, but by your own (periodic) contributions.

Note: Money that you already have in your bank account (or any non-registered investments) is not taxable. Only the income you get from it (interest or dividends or capital gain from the investment) is taxable.

If you have an RRSP, your withdrawals from it will be added to the other sources of income, and it will be taxed at the same rate as your salary.

Old Age Security

The Old Age Security (OAS) pension is a monthly payment available to most seniors aged 65 and older.

To qualify for maximum OAS, you have to live in Canada for at least 40 years after turning 18. For now you can apply when you turn 65 years old. However, if you are born after 1957, OAS eligibility age is 67 years old. Please visit http://artemfinancial.ca/links/oas-born-1958 for more information.

The maximum Old Age Security is $558 per month (for 2014). Most people get the maximum because it is based solely on residency.

If your total gross income is more than the threshold of $70,954 (2014), you might lose some of your OAS due to "clawback," which means that for every dollar of income above $70,954, the amount of OAS is reduced by 15 cents. When a pensioner's net income is $114,815 or above, they are not eligible to receive OAS.

The maximum OAS and the thresholds are adjusted yearly (and they usually increase with inflation). You can choose to delay receiving your OAS pension for up to 5 years (currently, the rule is until you are 70 years old). For every month you delay your OAS pension, you will receive an increased monthly pension of 0.6% per month up to a maximum of 36% at the age of 70. Please refer to http://artemfinancial.ca/links/deferring-oas for more information.

Please refer to http://artemfinancial.ca/links/oas to learn more about OAS and payment structure.

Canada Pension Plan or Québec Pension Plan

The Canada Pension Plan (CPP) operates throughout Canada, except Quebec where the Québec Pension Plan (QPP) provides corresponding benefits. CPP pays a monthly retirement pension to people who have worked and contributed to the CPP. The best way to figure out how much CPP you qualify for is to get your CPP "statement of contributions," which you can request by calling Service Canada at 1-800-277-9914. They will provide you with access to your online statement. You can choose to begin to receive CPP anywhere between 60 and 70 years old. The maximum benefit at age 65 is $1,038 per month (for 2014), but most people will receive less than that.

Your monthly CPP amount will increase by a certain percentage if you choose to start it after age 65.

Your monthly CPP amount will decrease by a certain percentage if you choose to start it before age 65.

This amount is adjusted yearly (and it again usually increases with inflation). The amount you receive depends on how long you worked and how much you (and your employer) contributed between the ages of 18 and 65 (or till you retire if that happens before 65 years old). If you are self-employed, you have to make contribution for yourself and for your employer.

If you are under 65 and you work while receiving your CPP retirement pension, you and your employer have to make CPP contributions, which will increase your CPP retirement benefits. Again, if you are self-employed, you have to contribute for both.

If you are between 65 and 70 years old and you work while receiving your CPP retirement pension, you may choose to make CPP contributions, which will again increase your CPP retirement benefits.

Please refer to http://artemfinancial.ca/links/cpp to learn more.

QPP (Québec Pension Plan) operates similarly, but it has its own unique features. For information about the QPP, please visit http://artemfinancial.ca/links/qpp.

There are two other forms of CPP payment: the disability payment and the survivor payment. The disability payment can come into effect if you are completely unable to work regularly due to disability. The survivor payments include a one-time payment to the estate of the contributor, as well as monthly payments to the spouse or common-law partner, and to dependent children.

You can fill out an estimate CPP form to find out how much your CPP will be; please visit http://artemfinancial.ca/links/estimate-cpp.

Additional monthly benefits for Old Age Security pensioners

The GIS (Guaranteed Income Supplement), Allowance, and Allowance for the Survivor are additional monthly benefits for low-income OAS pensioners. A person qualifying for GIS or Allowance typically has a very low income and does not have (or has very few) investments. To be eligible for the GIS benefit, you must be receiving the Old Age Security pension, meet the income requirements, and meet other criteria.

The GIS and Allowance are not taxable income, and therefore they do not matter for your decisions regarding your RRSP contributions. However, you must still report this income when you file your tax return.

To get more information about GIS, Allowance, and Allowance for the Survivor, please consult the following Service Canada links:

- **GIS** at http://artemfinancial.ca/links/gis

- **Allowance** at http://artemfinancial.ca/links/allowance

- **Allowance for the Survivor** at http://artemfinancial.ca/links/allowance-survivor

The Government of Canada has proposed to gradually increase the age of eligibility for the OAS pension and the Guaranteed Income Supplement (GIS) from 65 to 67, between the years 2023 and 2029. The Government of Canada also proposed to gradually increase the ages at which the Allowance and the Allowance for the Survivor are provided, from 60–64 today to 62–66 in the future.

Individuals currently receiving OAS benefits will not be affected by the proposed changes.

To conclude, if your anticipated income (including OAS/CPP) at the age of 65 is about the same as your current taxable income, then contributing to an RRSP is probably not a good retirement strategy. It is worth mentioning again that if your employer matches your RRSP contribution, then you should still contribute to an RRSP, regardless of your anticipated OAS/CPP.

Spousal RRSP

A spousal RRSP is where one spouse makes an RRSP contribution, but the other spouse owns the plan. This only makes sense if one spouse generates significantly more income than the other.

This strategy provides a means of income splitting. With income splitting, both retired spouses will have approximately the same income, which will reduce their total income tax. In a spousal RRSP, the spouse with a higher income (i.e. the spousal RRSP contributor) will contribute to the plan, and they can then claim a tax deduction. For all intents and purposes, the money within the spousal RRSP will now belong to the lower income spouse. The main caveat is that the higher income spouse will be taxed if the lower income spouse withdraws from the plan within the next two full calendar years after the last contribution (in other words, you have to wait for December 31 three times after the last contribution). If withdrawal takes place after this period, the lower income spouse will be taxed.

It is not necessary to set up a spousal RRSP account just because two spouses are in different tax brackets. For example, it is possible that a higher earning spouse has no pension, but the lower income spouse has a great future pension. In this case, it might be better for the higher income spouse to just contribute to their own RRSP so that their RRSP or RRIF income will be approximately equivalent to the other spouse's defined benefit pension income. The goal is income equalization.

Group RRSP

A group registered retirement savings plan (as mentioned above) is similar to an individual RRSP, but your employer administers it (through a designated administrator) on a group basis.

Employee contributions are often matched by the employer, up to a certain limit. Employer contributions are viewed as the employee's income, and they are therefore taxable. However, employees receive RRSP contribution slips, which make them eligible for deductions, offsetting the taxable benefit from the employer.

Registered Retirement Income Fund or Life Income Fund

There are many similar types of retirement income funds, including LRIF (locked-in retirement income fund), LIF (life income fund), and RLIF (restricted life income fund). Since the LIF is the most popular program, other programs are not discussed in this book. LIFs are available in all jurisdictions except in PEI.

A RRIF/LIF is the opposite of an RRSP/LIRA. RRSP/LIRA are programs you contribute into, while RRIF/LIF are programs you withdraw money from.

To open a RRIF/LIF you have to have an RRSP/LIRA to begin with. There is no tax consequence when you transfer money from an RRSP to a RRIF or from a LIRA to a LIF.

The difference between a RRIF and a LIF/LRIF is that a RRIF is used to transfer individual RRSP assets and an LRIF/LIF is used to transfer employer sponsored pension assets.

You do not need to retire to withdraw money from your RRSP/RRIF. However, the LIRA/LIF programs are different.

Two major differences between RRIFs and LIFs

1. The amount that can be withdrawn from a RRIF has a minimum but no maximum, while a LIF has both a minimum (the same as for RRIF) and a maximum. The maximum amounts are regulated by federal or provincial pension legislation. If your LIF is regulated federally, you can get the maximum withdrawal from the Office of the Superintendent of Financial Institutions (http://artemfinancial.ca/links/osfi-lif). For provincially regulated funds, follow the links from TaxTips site table of RPP regulators (http://artemfinancial.ca/links/pension-regulators).

2. A RRIF does not have any age restriction; you can convert your RRSP to a RRIF at any age (but see below). Conversely, you can convert your LIRA to a LIF (and subsequently withdraw the funds from LIF) only when you get to "retirement age" (which depends on LIRA legislation). There are two common exceptions for when you can convert LIRA to LIF before retirement age: in these cases, you should prove financial hardship or shortened life expectancy.

Before the age of 71, you can have RRSP and/or RRIFs. Starting the first January 1 after you turn 71, you are no longer allowed to have RRSPs, and you have three options instead:

1. Convert all of your RRSPs to RRIFs.

2. Withdraw all of your money from your RRSPs directly.

3. Buy an annuity (see the explanation of RRSP withdrawal).

Once you open a RRIF, you have to withdraw at least the minimum amount every year (starting the withdrawal the following year after you open a RRIF). If you choose to withdraw from the RRIF the same year you opened it, this would be the same as withdrawing money directly from an RRSP, i.e. you will pay the same withholding tax (see RRSP withholding tax in the RRSP discussion).

If you are not yet 71 years old, you can convert your RRIF back to an RRSP and stop withdrawing money from it.

The point of converting your RRSP to a RRIF before the age of 71 is to get income starting next year. For example, you know that you will not work next year and you will need some income, so you can convert some of your RRSP, or all of it, to a RRIF, receive the needed income and then convert that money back to RRSP when you have other sources of income.

You can have as many RRIF accounts as you wish, but you will have to withdraw at least the minimum amount from each one of them.

The minimum is calculated each year as a percentage of the plan's total value on January 1.

Before the age of 71, the RRIF minimum withdrawal is calculated in the following way:

(the market value of the RRIF balance) x [1/(90 - plan holder's age)]

After the age of 71, the calculation is different. At the age of 71 you have to withdraw at least 7.38% from each of your RRIF plans.

When you only withdraw the minimum from your RRIF or LIF, you do not need to pay tax at the time of withdrawal.

If you withdraw more than the minimum, you pay withholding tax on the excess of the minimum (withholding tax will be the same as when you withdraw money from RRSP directly).

You decide when you want to withdraw money, and you can do it periodically or as a lump sum.

Minimum RRIF Withdrawals

Age on Jan 1	Min Amount	Age on Jan 1	Min Amount
65	4.00%	80	8.75%
66	4.17%	81	8.99%
67	4.35%	82	9.27%
68	4.55%	83	9.58%
69	4.76%	84	9.93%
70	5.00%	85	10.33%
71	7.38%	86	10.79%
72	7.48%	87	11.33%
73	7.59%	88	11.96%
74	7.71%	89	12.71%
75	7.85%	90	13.62%
76	7.99%	91	14.73%
77	8.15%	92	16.12%
78	8.33%	93	17.92%
79	8.53%	94	20.00%

TIP 44
Transfer your RRSP to a RRIF

At the age of 65, transfer some of your RRSP to a RRIF (consult your accountant as to exactly how much to transfer) and take $2,000 out per year from age 65 to 71 (inclusive). This strategy allows you to get $2,000 out of your RRSP tax-free (or to pay very little tax) for several years.

One of the biggest risks associated with having registered programs that nobody talks about is investment options risk.

When the government is desperate to raise money, it can change the law and require all registered program holders to have certain investments, for example, government bonds.

It has happened many times in the history of many countries, and holders of such programs could not do much other than comply with the new law.

Obviously, such law will not be in favour of account holders. It will have very serious financial consequences for the country, and so it has little chance of being implemented.

However, the risk exists.

RRSP and RRIF beneficiaries

Beneficiary is spouse or disabled child or dependent child below 18
• No taxes if transferred to spouse's RRSP; dependent children pay taxes or can buy annuity.
Other beneficiaries
• Beneficiaries receive the assets but taxes are paid by estate.
No beneficiary
• Assets are paid to the estate, all the debts are paid off, and the assets are taxed after that.
• With a will: the rest is distributed as per will.
• Without a will: the rest is distributed as per law.

You can designate a beneficiary in your RRSP (or Spousal RRSP). This has the following advantages:

- Naming your spouse as your beneficiary (which is the most common selection) has tax benefits.

- If you designate your friend, relative, or children as your beneficiary(ies), the RRSP will be distributed as per your designation, but taxes will be paid by the estate. (Note that if you wish to designate your children as your beneficiaries, they should be at the age of majority.)

Example: Child Beneficiary for RRSP

If you have an RRSP and you designate your child as your beneficiary, the child will receive the RRSP in full, but income tax will have to be paid from your other assets (the RRSP is not part of your estate in this case because you designated your child to be your beneficiary).

If nobody pays income tax on the disposition of the RRSP, then CRA will come after your child to pay it.

When no beneficiary is designated in the RRSP account agreement, the Canada Revenue Agency (CRA) determines that the deceased annuitant's estate is automatically the beneficiary of the RRSP assets. With no designated beneficiary, the RRSP assets will be considered the property of the estate and distributed as dictated by your will.

You can change your beneficiary(ies) at any time, and different plans can have different beneficiaries.

You should designate your spouse or common-law spouse as a successor annuitant in the RRIF (instead of a beneficiary).

If a successor annuitant was designated, they will receive the remaining RRIF payments, and they do not need to make any changes to the deceased's RRIF investments.

If there is no successor annuitant, the deceased person's RRIF will be closed causing a disposition of all investments in the RRIF, followed by a rollover to an RRSP or RRIF of the surviving spouse.

If there was no successor designated, the disadvantages are:

- It may not be a good time to sell the investments.

- There may be selling costs.

- There may be a lot of paperwork to complete.

If you make a mistake and name the spouse as a beneficiary, the CRA will probably interpret that as meaning "successor annuitant." You can designate beneficiaries in your RRIF at any time, as well.

Rules differ in Quebec: beneficiary designations are not recognized and assets should be distributed through wills. Thus, for a RRIF, a spouse should be named as a "successor annuitant" in the will.

Similarly, Yukon residents cannot make RRIF designations.

When you convert your RRSP or LIRA to a RRIF or LIF, you set up a new contract, and you must designate a beneficiary at that time; your previous RRSP or LIRA designations will not apply any more.

Chapter 11 notes

Please use this space for your notes.

Chapter 12: HOW TO IMPROVE YOUR RETIREMENT CASH FLOW

If you are 55 years of age or older, the Pension Income Tax credit is available to you.

It enables you to deduct, from taxes that you pay, a tax credit equal to the lesser of your pension incomes or $2,000. Depending on which province you live in, this could add up to $700 in actual tax savings each year.

The pension income tax credit is non-refundable and may not be carried forward each year, which means that you need to use it if you can, or you lose it.

To claim the credit, the taxpayer must be in receipt of certain specified income. Eligible pension income depends on your age.

If you are younger than 65 on December 31, your eligible pension income for that year includes:

- income from a superannuation or pension plan

- annuity income arising from the death of your spouse under RRSP, RRIF, or DPSP (Deferred Profit Sharing Plan)

If you are 65 or older in the current calendar year, your eligible pension income for that year includes:

- income from a superannuation or pension fund

- annuity income out of an RRSP or a DPSP

- income from a RRIF

- interest from a prescribed non-registered annuity

- income from foreign pensions

- interest from a non-registered GIC offered by a life insurance company

Non-eligible pension income sources are:

- investment income from market based investments (i.e. stocks, mutual funds)

- interest income from a GIC with banks, trust companies, and credit unions

- OAS or CPP or GIS

- lump sum death benefits

- lump sum withdrawals from RRSP

- retiring allowances (please visit http://artemfinancial.ca/links/retiring-allowances for more information)

If you are over 65 years old and you are not part of a superannuation or pension plan, you may be able to create eligible pension income to save on taxes.

Income splitting strategies available for retirees:

- pension splitting

- CPP or QPP splitting

CPP or QPP splitting applies to income from CPP or QPP, while pension splitting applies to eligible pension income (which does not include CPP).

Pension splitting

Pension splitting allows a spouse to give up to 50% of their eligible pension income to their spouse for tax purposes. Splitting is done via spouses' tax returns.

While payments received from RRIF are considered eligible pension income for income splitting purposes, RRSP withdrawals are not. CPP or QPP and OAS income are also not eligible for pension splitting.

CPP or QPP splitting

A CPP or QPP splitting strategy makes sense when one spouse receives higher CPP or QPP payments and is in a higher tax bracket than the other spouse. Both spouses must be over the age of 60, and both must be collecting CPP or QPP.

Example: CPP splitting

If the higher income spouse earns $900 per month and the other spouse earns $100 per month, a CPP or QPP split allows each spouse to take $500 per month. You and your partner must make a joint choice in CRA form T1032 (form RRQ-060 in Quebec).

Some differences between pension splitting and CPP or QPP splitting:

- Pension splitting is a one-directional split, which means that one spouse can give the second spouse up to half of his or her pension income with no expectation of returned income.

  CPP is a two-directional split, which means that one spouse can give the second spouse half of his or her CPP, but the second spouse must also give half of his or her CPP to the first spouse. In the same example, if the higher income spouse earns $900 per month and the other spouse earns $100 per month, a CPP or QPP split allows each spouse to take $500 per month: $900/2 + $100/2.

- Pension splitting can happen as soon as you collect pension income (in most cases, at the age of 55).

  With pension splitting, there is no application process. Splitting is done via tax returns, and thus the amount of pension being split is determined by the taxpayer, not the government or anyone else.

  The spouse receiving the pension does not have to be at a certain age to receive pension income through pension splitting.

- You must apply for CPP splitting through an application process. You can also apply to un-split CPP. To apply, both spouses must be over the age of 60 and both must have applied to collect CPP. In most cases, the split is 50/50, but in some cases (as in second or third marriages), the split may not be 50/50.

- With CPP splitting, there is a physical distribution of benefits, which means that both spouses get cheques or deposits with equal amounts.

- With pension splitting, one spouse does not give the other one any cash. The transfer is a paper transaction done on tax forms.

Property tax deferment programs

According to most provincial or municipal laws, "house-rich" seniors (seniors who own property but have few other assets) in need of extra cash can have their property taxes deferred until they either pass away or sell their house (or receive discounts). Please refer to the appropriate provincial sites below, based on your province or city of residence.

- **BC**: http://artemfinancial.ca/links/tax-deferral-bc

- **Alberta**: http://artemfinancial.ca/links/tax-deferral-ab

- **Saskatoon**: http://artemfinancial.ca/links/tax-deferral-sc

- **Halifax**: http://artemfinancial.ca/links/tax-deferral-halifax

- **Nova Scotia**: http://artemfinancial.ca/links/tax-deferral-ns

- **Ontario**: http://artemfinancial.ca/links/tax-deferral-on

- **Ottawa**: http://artemfinancial.ca/links/tax-deferral-ottawa

- **PEI**: http://artemfinancial.ca/links/tax-deferral-pei

The Canada Pension Plan Child-Rearing Provision (CPP CRP)

You should request the child-rearing provision if you stopped working or received lower earnings while caring for your children under 7 years old. Applying for CRP may increase the amount of your CPP benefit. Please refer to http://artemfinancial.ca/links/child-rearing-provision for more information.

Reverse mortgages

A reverse mortgage is a type of mortgage whose goal is to generate income for a senior aged 55 years or older who has equity in his or her home.

A reverse mortgage is a loan which you take using your home as collateral. There are no payments on this type of loan, but the interest on the loan accumulates, decreasing the equity that you have in your home.

If you receive OAS or GIS, a reverse mortgage will not affect them.

This loan is not taxable, and you can use it for investment purposes or for personal consumption. In this case of an investment loan, the interest on the reverse mortgage might be tax deductible (depending what investments you buy).

Consider a reverse mortgage, in particular, if you do not have or do not intend to have beneficiaries.

Before applying for a reverse mortgage, you should get independent advice.

At the time of writing, there is only one company providing reverse mortgages, the Canadian Home Income Plan (CHIP). Please visit http://artemfinancial.ca/links/chip for more information.

Please refer to the sites for the Financial Consumer Agency of Canada – FCAC (http://artemfinancial.ca/links/reverse-mortgage1) and the Canada Mortgage and Housing Corporation – CMHC (http://artemfinancial.ca/links/reverse-mortgage) to get more information about reverse mortgages.

Defined benefit and defined contribution plans

Some companies offer some kind of pension for their employees. Usually there are two types of these benefits: defined benefit and defined contribution.

Defined Benefit Pension Plan (DB)

The DB income you receive at retirement is determined in advance, and it normally follows a formula involving your years of work and income within this company.

To put it differently, DB is monthly pension from your employer when you retire. DB can be contributory or non-contributory.

Contributory DB means that the employee has to make contributions to the plan, and the employer can match these contributions.

Non-contributory DB means that only the employer makes contributions. Under a DB plan, a financial institution designated by your employer manages the assets, and you are not involved in investment decisions. When you pass away, the pension ceases (in some cases your spouse can continue to receive it).

Defined Contribution Pension Plan (DC)

The DC income is not known in advance but is based on the assets in your individual retirement plan. In a DC plan, your employer contributes to the plan, and you may or may not be required to make any contributions.

The formula for these contributions usually involves a fixed percentage of your salary or a specific amount.

In a DC, you (or your advisor) determine which investments your contributions are invested in, choosing from a selection of investment options available within your DC plan.

You are the decision maker, and you invest the money as you wish (or as per your advisor's recommendation).

You can designate a beneficiary that will receive assets from the plan after you pass away.

Most Canadian pension plans are DC plans, because employers tend to avoid taking responsibility for pensions for their employees.

The employee's RRSP contribution room is reduced when contributions are made to DB or DC, regardless of who (i.e. employer and/or employee) made the contribution.

The employee's contributions are tax deductible (i.e. they will decrease your income by the amount contributed). The employer's contributions are neither tax deductible nor taxable to you.

DC and DB plans may normally be transferred to another financial institution when you switch to another employer (the transferred money often becomes LIRA).

Annuities

An annuity has fixed payments over a specified period of time. Since these payments do not come from investments, they do not depend on any market and are therefore guaranteed. Only insurance companies sell annuities.

Different types of annuities are offered by different insurance companies. Life and term annuities are among the most common types. A life annuity provides you with guaranteed fixed payments until you pass away.

- **Life Annuity** can be based on just your life, or be a joint and survivor with somebody else (e.g. spouse).

- **Term Annuity** provides you with guaranteed fixed payments for a certain period of time. The longer the period, the smaller the payments, everything else being equal.

**TIP 45
Annuities tie up your cash**

When you buy an annuity, your decision is irrevocable. Do not put too much of your capital into an annuity: it can provide a good cash flow, but your capital will be gone.

TIP 46
When annuities can be good investments

An annuity is a good investment when interest rates are high (as they were in the 1980s) and they are going down. It is a bad investment when interest rates are low and they are going up. There are two reasons for that.

First, annuity payments are based on the interest at the time when you sign the contract. The lower the interest, the lower the payments you will receive.

Second, inflation and (as a result) interest rates may start to go up, but you might be only indexed (i.e. inflation-protected) up to a certain limit.

When is a good time to buy an annuity? It might be a good idea to watch the price of gold for an answer. The price of gold is going up when the Real Interest Rate is negative (Real Interest Rate = Nominal Interest Rate minus Inflation) i.e. the inflation is higher than the interest you can get, for example, on a savings account or on Government bonds.

When the Real Interest Rate is positive and the price of gold is falling, it might be a good time to buy annuities. Interest rates usually move in very long cycles which last about 30 years. Currently, interest rates are among the lowest they've ever been and they will go up eventually. The next time you should buy annuities might be decades from now.

Registered annuities are annuities that are purchased with "registered savings" funds. Registered savings funds include any funds accumulated in RRIFs, LIRAs, RRSPs or LIFs (it does not make much sense to have annuities in an RRSP, but this option is also available). For registered annuities for accounts mentioned above, all payments are considered to be income, and they are fully taxable.

Non-registered annuities are bought with funds from "non-registered" savings. Payments from non-registered annuities are only partly taxable, since they include partial return of capital.

The two biggest problems with annuities are inflation and outliving your money (if you buy term annuities).

Since you receive a constant stream of income, the value of this income can (and probably will) diminish because of inflation. Some annuities can be indexed to offset inflation, but usually they are indexed on a lower basis than the real rate of inflation. Once an annuity is bought, it is final: you cannot re-sell your annuity contract to get a lump sum back.

Universal Life Insurance

If you have maximized your RRSP and TFSA contributions and you are looking for an investment that can grow tax-free, you may want to consider universal life insurance.

This type of insurance has two components: life insurance and investment. Investments grow tax sheltered till you withdraw them (if at all). Cash can be withdrawn at any time, subject to policy rules.

Another advantage of universal life insurance is protection of assets from creditors. Universal life insurance is sold by insurance companies only. In most cases, it is appropriate to use a universal life insurance investment component only after TFSA/RRSP contributions are maximized.

Universal life insurance is a very complicated product. However, it is a very good tool for estate planning, and the investment component helps transfer your wealth, tax free, to anyone you choose.

TIP 47
Gold prices vary with the economy

Gold is not an inflation protection, and the 1980s are a good example of this. In the 1980s, North America experienced a very high rate of inflation, but the price of gold went down. The reason is that the Real Interest Rate was still positive, and there was no point to investing in gold if you could get a higher than inflation rate on something else, e.g. Government bonds or GIC.

Chapter 12 notes

Please use this space for your notes.

Chapter 13: IDENTITY THEFT, SCAMS, AND WAYS TO PROTECT YOURSELF

Unfortunately, if your identity is stolen, it is very difficult to fix the situation. It takes a lot of time and money, and can even prevent you from finding a job (since employers may want to know how good/bad your credit history is).

More and more people suffer from identity theft and have to fix their credit history. In many cases, people learn that their identity has been compromised only months if not years after the fact.

Here are some measures you can take to prevent your own identity being stolen. Thieves are looking for easy targets, and they do not want to be caught. Remember, if you do not care about your data, thieves will.

1. Never throw your mail away. Instead, always destroy it (e.g. with a shredder).

2. Try to get as many online bills as possible. This way you do not receive any mail, and thieves will not know your name and address.

3. Always check transactions on your credit and/or debit card bill(s). Thieves will not buy expensive items; they are satisfied with small transactions which most people will not notice. Always report such transactions and immediately change your card(s).

4. Never use the same password for different accounts (i.e. email account password should be different from your bank account password). Never use simple passwords because it takes only about 7 minutes to break a relatively simple password (please refer to the article at http://artemfinancial.ca/links/passw-and-nsa).

   There are many storage password programs you can use to store all of your passwords and usernames (and many such programs are free to use, for example, Keepass at http://artemfinancial.ca/links/store-passw). You need to remember only one password to access the program. The program and the file with passwords will be stored on your computer, and nobody except you will have access to it.

This way you can use different and complex passwords for different purposes, and you do not need to remember your username and password each time.

Some programs even generate random passwords if you cannot create them on your own. Even if your computer has been hacked or stolen, nobody will be able to access this program without your password to this software.

5. Always save and/or make copies of all your important information and documents, e.g. IDs, credit and debit card numbers, account numbers, addresses, and telephone numbers. Make backups of your cell phone, smart phone, and computers.

6. Never save your backup on your computer, as there is no point to making a backup of your computer and keeping it there. For your backup you can use a memory stick, a portable disk, or even internet backup sites (some of them offer free storage, for example, Cyphertite at http://artemfinancial.ca/links/cyphertite).

   It might be a good idea not to keep your backup at your home, in case fire or theft happen. Open a safe deposit box with a bank or give it to your friend, relative, or any other person you fully trust.

   If you use internet backup sites, make sure that they encrypt the data before uploading the data to their site. This is very important because you do not want the employees of this internet site to have access to your private data. Some sites can do backups automatically on a daily/weekly/monthly basis (Cyphertite offers all of that).

7. Make sure you can access this site from another city or country, in case of emergency. If you keep a file with passwords (as described above) on a backup site, make sure you also upload the program that can open that file. If the company that created the password software ceases to exist or upgrades their software, your file with passwords might not be accessible. Do not use Word or Excel documents to store your credit card information, as they can be easily accessed or hacked.

8. Some credit card companies – if you have a credit card with them – can notify you when a financial institution inquires about your credit history.

If you have not applied for credit yourself, you will immediately know that someone is probably trying to steal your identity.

9. Never give your social insurance number to anyone unless you have to (e.g. your bank or the CRA).

10. Do not trust phone calls, especially if someone calls you, claims that they represent an institution you deal with, and asks you to provide additional information or confirm some old information. Take the name of the person and call this person back by dialling the generic institution's number rather than the number this individual gave you. If you are afraid of looking silly when asking the name and telling the person you will call back, think of how silly you will look if it is an actual scam.

11. Never make decisions immediately. If someone you do not know tells you that you need to invest, give them money, or act immediately, it could be a scam.

    To check this, you can tell the individual that you want to take some information with you and consult with your brother who works at Ontario Securities Commission. You do not need to have a brother (or a brother who works there), but if you say this on the telephone, you will learn if it is a scam immediately.

12. Since we are all emotional beings, we adjust facts to our beliefs. If you like an investment option that is presented to you (which could be a scam), you will justify to yourself why certain things that do not readily make sense (to a rational person) are very attractive. It is very important to question your beliefs and get a second opinion or even entertain the possibility of you being wrong. It is better to lose an opportunity than to lose money with this opportunity. You might have another opportunity, but you cannot get back the money you have lost.

13. If your identity has been stolen, notify Equifax and TransUnion about it. Make sure that your report has been updated by requesting your credit report from them in a month. It might be a good idea to contact the police and change your SIN, using a police report.

14. Consider getting a mail box from the nearest UPS store or another provider who can give you a physical mailing address (and not a P.O. box like Canada Post offers). Get all your mail there. It is much more difficult to steal your identity if the thieves do not know your home address. If you have to mail someone something, do not write your home address as your return address, but use either your work address or mailing address instead.

15. Never send emails with your important information (such as SIN or a credit card number) to anyone, since emails can be broken into and you might not even know that your information has been stolen.

16. Always make sure your computer is protected by an antivirus and/or firewall program. It must not be free software, and it must be up to date.

17. If you leave your computer for repair, make sure you do not have any data that can be compromised. Even if you leave it with a trustworthy company, you never know exactly who will have access to your data.

18. Never assume that a smiling person has good intentions. Bad guys rarely look gloomy, since they will do everything they can for people to like and trust them.

    On the other hand, do not assume that if a person does not smile, they are not friendly. In some cultures, people smile when they want to laugh and not when they meet other people for business.

19. If you need someone to do some (contract) work for you, always prepare contracts, write down what the responsibilities of this individual are, and always mention privacy and confidentiality in the contract. The person you hire has to sign the contract. Do not forget to verify his or her ID(s).

    There are two reasons to sign a contract. First, you need to make sure that the person does the work they are hired for.

    Second, if the person has bad intentions, they will think well before implementing them. If they do not sign any contracts, they might not be liable for a fraud or for disclosing information, etc.

Many internet sites may help you generate simple contracts including (among other things) a confidentiality clause. Make sure the site you use provides contracts suitable for Canadian laws and that the generated contract is valid in Canada and in your province of residence, more specifically.

20. Try to avoid withdrawing money from ATMs that do not belong to a known bank or a credit union. Your debit card information can be copied and compromised.

21. Always notify your credit card company when you leave for a trip to another province or country.

22. Make sure you have an extra credit card in case your primary credit card has been compromised and you have to wait till you get a replacement. This is especially important when going abroad.

23. Never use public computers (i.e. airport, library, internet café, etc.) to access sites with your personal information. If you have to use a public computer, find a "virtual keyboard" site (search "online virtual keyboard" in Google, for example). The idea is that you do not use the actual keyboard provided with the public computer, but click letters on a virtual keyboard using the mouse. You can then copy and paste the whole username/password to log into a site of your choice. This way, if the public computer has a virus that records everything typed on the physical keyboard, your username/password will not be compromised because you haven't used the actual keyboard.

24. If you receive an unexpected email with great news (such as winning a lottery or the price of a specific stock will go up in 3 days), this is a scam. Do not reply to the email.

25. If you do not want the tellers of your bank to access your accounts, some banks offer extra privacy protection where tellers are not able to see what you have, but only the manager (usually the branch manager) has access to all your accounts. It is not a very popular and common feature for a bank to offer as it slows your banking significantly (because, if the manager is busy or out of office, tellers will not be able to help you at all), but it provides an additional level of privacy.

26. If you receive an email that asks you to log in to your bank account or another personal account, this is probably a phishing email (to learn more, please read the article at http://artemfinancial.ca/links/phishing).

    If you want to check the legitimacy of the request without any risk, go directly to your own online login without clicking the suspicious link – it may contain malware.

    You can also contact your bank or credit card company directly. There are several ways to check that. You can hover over the link of this email (do not click it) and make sure that the URL address of the site (i.e. web address) starts with HTTPS (and not with HTTP). The letter "S" in HTTPS stands for "security" and (to make a long explanation short) HTTPS provides authentication of the website and encryption of your personal information (like username/password, etc.).

    Thieves do not use HTTPS for their fake sites. Also, make sure that the URL address of the website corresponds to the actual site the email wants you to go to: no bank will use "http://go.to" or a similar site without the company name in the web address.

27. Another way to check if this email is legitimate is, of course, to call the company it claims to be emailed from. Never call the number from the email itself, but find the telephone number from the company's website.

28. Request your credit history reports from the credit agencies every year (at the very least) and verify all the information the reports contain. Reports are free to order if they are physically mailed. Checking reports every year might save you from troubles.

29. If you are a sophisticated internet user, you can consider using VPN (Virtual Private Network). Please read the article at http://artemfinancial.ca/links/vpn to learn more.

    There are many VPN providers, that will charge you from $5 per month or more, and it will help you avoid being watched by many organizations that collect data about you while you use internet (please read the article

"What Google Knows About You" at http://artemfinancial.ca/links/google-knows-you).

A VPN will slow down your internet, but you do not need to use VPN all the time: you can turn it on only when you need extra privacy.

30. Most internet browsers have the option of switching to a "browse privately" setting (each browser has its own name but the idea is the same). You will access internet privately, and the browser will not store your personal data. It is not very convenient because the browser will not store your usernames and history of browsed sites (among other things), but it is a good idea if you want to do something and do not want anyone to know what you did (access your bank account, for example). This does not replace VPN service.

31. There are many (free) add-ons you can add to your browser that will prevent or disable ads, banners, and scripts that can act as viruses and/or collect your private information. Your computer's antivirus software probably cannot deal with such internet scripts.

32. If you do not mind spending some money to protect yourself from identity theft, Equifax and TransUnion offer identity theft protection plans and insurance.

33. If you use social media sites such as Facebook or Google Plus, turn off the option that can identify your location and do not make your profile public.

34. If you want to buy something on the internet and you do not want anyone to know about this, do not use your personal credit or debit card, since the transaction will be visible to the employees of the credit card company or bank (and even to your spouse if you share the same credit card or account). To protect your privacy, use prepaid cards or gift credit cards that cannot be traced back to you. Preventive measures are much cheaper than what you have to deal with after the fact.

Chapter 13 notes

Please use this space for your notes.

Chapter 14: HOW TO SAVE MONEY

Why do you need to save money?

When you save money, you save your own time, which you need to earn that money.

Example: Save More Than You Earn

If you earn $30/hr and you have saved $20 by not buying something or buying the product cheaper, then you have actually saved about 1 hour of your time ($20 after tax is about $30 before tax plus unemployment insurance plus CPP/QPP contributions).

Time is your most valuable resource. When you want to spend money, think that what you actually spend is your time. The same logic applies when you decide to spend your time on something that can be done by a professional who (perhaps) gets paid less than you do and does the job more efficiently.

Many items that people own cost not just the initial price paid for them but also the maintenance cost, as well. Consider these:

- The fewer vehicles you own, the less insurance and maintenance you pay.
- The fewer TVs or computers you own, the less electricity you consume.
- The more houses you own (for your own use and not for investment purposes), the more property taxes, maintenance, and insurance you will pay.

The outcome is simple: the more items you own, the more time you need to work to pay for these items' maintenance and the less time you have for your own life.

Many people consider frugality to be a bad thing. Nothing could be further from the truth. Our resources such as time, money, and water are limited, and if we waste them thoughtlessly, we will be left without them. Simply do not listen to people who say that you have to have a bigger or newer XYZ (replace XYZ with an item). You know better.

Martin E. P. Seligman, who wrote *Authentic Happiness* (http://artemfinancial. ca/links/book-happiness), has shown that to be happy you do not need to be rich or have a lot of "toys." People in poorer countries are much happier as a rule than people in countries with a much higher standard of living.

Money Saving Ideas

1. Canadians like to spend money, and the most expensive item they buy is their home.

    *   It is not just the home itself but everything you buy and pay for after you buy your home: appliances, furniture, renovations, insurance, maintenance, property taxes, etc.

    *   The bigger the home you have, the greater the bills that you receive.

    *   Downsizing or buying a house that you really can afford can contribute a lot to your financial future.

    *   Thomas Stanley, the author of *The Millionaire Next Door* (http:// artemfinancial.ca/links/m-next-door), argues that overspending on the personal home is the biggest factor that contributes to failing to achieve financial freedom.

    *   Make sure that you own your house and not the other way around.

2. Many big grocery stores open at 6 a.m. or 7 a.m., and if you go there at that time you will be able to save on gas (less traffic on the roads), and in many cases you will be able to buy products that expire soon and are sold with a 30–50% discount.

3. Many consumers are misled into thinking that expired products are rotten or spoiled after the expiry date, contrary to fact. The expiry date is merely the manufacturer's recommendation as to when the product's quality is at its best (hence the "best before" label on many products rather than the "expiry date" label). In reality, many products are likely to be in perfect to good condition days and even weeks after they expire (not to mention that

most expired frozen products could still be good months after the "best before" date).

4. To save time and money, do not go shopping on weekends. On Mondays and Tuesdays, most stores often offer the best deals because they are restocked after the weekend, and they need to get rid of unsold products left from the weekend. Not to mention that when you go shopping during week days, you can find what you need rather than empty shelves.

5. Always create a list of items you need to buy. Do not just browse the store; go directly to the shelf that has the item you want. Stores often rearrange their products to make sure that you go through everywhere to find what you want and buy what you might not really need.

6. Go shopping less often but when you do, go to all the stores in one trip to save on gas and time.

7. Usually gas prices go up before long weekends, so fill your tank before that. You may want to consider visiting http://artemfinancial.ca/links/cheap-gas to find the cheapest gas prices in your area.

8. When travelling long distance, do not drive faster than 90–100 km/h. Driving faster than that increases your vehicle's gas consumption significantly.

9. When your vehicle's air conditioning is running full, it can lower the fuel efficiency by 10–20%, depending on the type and age of your vehicle. However, though using the air conditioning does require your vehicle to burn more fuel, it is still more efficient than driving with the windows down. Putting the windows down increases drag on most cars, cancelling out the fuel efficiency gain from not running the air conditioning.

10. In summer, avoid driving during the hottest hours of the day to decrease air conditioning (and hence gas consumption).

11. Car roof racks increase gas consumption, so remove them when you are not using them.

12. Replace your air filter as recommended in your vehicle's manual. A clean air filter makes the car run more efficiently.

13. Align your tires and make sure that they are properly inflated. Proper alignment can boost fuel economy by 10%.

14. Do not idle your engine unnecessarily, and if you stop for more than just a couple of minutes (e.g. when you wait for a train to pass by), turn the engine off.

15. If you take a discount coupon for a certain product at a particular retail store, in many cases it will be valid at other stores, too, and in some stores the same item may be sold for a cheaper price.

16. Always check and compare prices on the shelves with your receipt right after the purchase. This thing alone will save you a lot of money. Canadian retailers are committed to accurate scanner pricing, so do not hesitate to consult the customer service desk even if the difference in price (not in your favour) is only one cent – you might get the item for free or might get a refund of $10. Please refer to http://artemfinancial.ca/links/price-accuracy or http://artemfinancial.ca/links/price-accuracy1. However, also consider how much time you will spend on this, compared to how much you are paid for your time at work.

17. Some credit cards offer purchase security and extended warranty. Purchase security insurance usually provides coverage for damage to the product purchased with the credit card. Extended warranty insurance extends the original manufacturer's warranty on the purchased product. Please check your insurance coverage with your credit card company.

Chapter 14 notes

Please use this space for your notes.

Chapter 15: HOW TO BUY (INVESTMENTS, VEHICLES, Etc.)

If you want to know why people want to sell you a specific item (an investment, a vehicle, etc.) you have to ask a simple question:

What are the seller's benefits when they sell this particular product rather than another (comparable) product?

People never ask this question, but the answer will help you identify what products you need to avoid. There are two possible answers to this question:

A. The salesperson gets paid for selling a particular product

If the benefit is financial, find out how much money (or what kind of benefit) the salesperson gets by selling other products. It is not always the price of the product that matters for the salesperson's benefit. Sometimes, the company wants to get rid of a specific item, and it might offer a better bonus or commission just to get this product completely removed from the shelves.

B. There is no financial benefit

If the benefit is not financial (the person is on salary and it does not matter to them what you buy as long as you buy something), ask the salesperson to tell you more about the items they did not offer. Some salespeople who do not get any sales commission are just lazy, and they want to sell products that sell easily, perhaps because they are easier to explain and understand, but they might not necessarily meet your needs.

To provide a financial example, GICs are easier to explain and understand than mutual funds. In case the salesperson does not receive any financial benefits, ask them about other products they sell and once they have explained them to you, they will not have any reason to offer an unsuitable product and so might change their advice.

How to buy or lease and maintain a car more cheaply

The following checklist can help you keep the costs of your vehicle under control. Consider each point. You might consider making some notes about how each has affected your recent vehicle.

1. When buying a car: whether you get financing from a dealer or from your bank, find out if your vehicle will be used as collateral. There is nothing wrong with this option, but it is something that is good to know in advance (since you will not be able to sell the vehicle as long as there is a lien on it).

2. When buying or leasing a car from a dealer: the farther away the dealer is from big cities, the cheaper your car might be because fewer people buy cars in small cities and dealers are ready to sell cars for less mark-up (i.e. profit). Always negotiate rather than accept the first price. Asking never hurts.

3. Do not lease a vehicle if you are going to drive it more than 20,000 to 22,000 km per year; driving more than that increases your leasing cost substantially.

4. Do not lease a car if you are planning to drive the car less than 15,000 km per year. Leasing is renting. If you rent something, you'd better use it; otherwise, you simply waste your money.

5. Do not buy from a dealer that does not specialize in the type of vehicle you intend to buy (e.g. a GM dealer selling VW cars). Such a dealer might not provide proper maintenance for the car, and you might buy a malfunctioning car.

6. Since many regions of Canada can be affected by flood, do not buy a car until it has been inspected by a qualified mechanic (and choose the mechanic yourself, rather than using one recommended by the seller). You might not see flood damage when you buy a car, but in case of an accident, the airbag might not open or something else might not work.

7. If you want to buy a car after you have leased it, check the value of the vehicle in the Black Book and compare it with what you have to pay. Do not buy if the Black Book value is significantly lower.

8. Never wash your car with dish soap because it will destroy the paint.

9. If you have bought or leased a brand new car, you probably automatically have roadside assistance from the car manufacturer. Purchase this assistance only if it is not included. Some credit cards offer roadside assistance as one of their insurance services.

10. If you want to sell your car, clean the inside and wax the outside. If you have had an accident, always tell this to your potential buyers before they ask. It is better to tell bad information upfront rather than wait until the buyer finds it out for themselves and decides not to trust you as a result. You could lose the sale.

11. Before you buy or lease a car, check how much car insurance will cost you. Similar models from different brands might have completely different insurance costs.

12. There are many internet sites where you can re-lease cars. Vehicles that are 3 or 4 years old have a much cheaper insurance cost but still benefit from the manufacturer's warranty. On top of that, people willing to get rid of their lease might offer you an additional incentive, e.g. pay for the lease for a couple of months or give you cash.

13. Read *Lemon Aid* by Phil Edmonston (http://artemfinancial.ca/links/lemon-aid) if you want to know more about how to buy and what to buy.

14. Most cars will drive perfectly well if you change oil after 7,000 or even 10,000 km. Changing oil after 5,000 km is often a waste of money; however, consult a qualified mechanic.

15. Find a good mechanic, and do not go to the car dealer. Most issues can be dealt with perfectly for much less money by good mechanics who do not work for the "brand."

16. If you have an accident, always document it by taking pictures. Most smart phones or cell phones are equipped with a camera, or you can buy a disposable camera and keep it in the car. It is much easier to submit a claim if you have proper evidence from the accident.

Chapter 15 notes

Please use this space for your notes.

SUMMARY

This section summarizes the main points of this book. Several pages are available for you to make notes of your own.

1. The biggest expense of your life is taxes. The CRA's job is to tax you. Your job (and the job of your advisors) is to save as much money from CRA as possible, legally, of course. We pay taxes on earned income and not on assets we own (with a few exceptions, such as land tax). Net income (income after taxes) is what is important, not gross income (income before tax).

2. Every investment decision has tax consequences, but the tax code is not always written based on logic. Do not assume that you know what your tax consequences will be. Research them thoroughly and/or consult a professional advisor.

3. You cannot achieve maximum tax savings without professional help: your accountant, financial planner, investment specialist, lawyer, or insurance advisor should help you. They should make or save you more money than what you pay them for their service. To distinguish the job of an accountant from that of a financial planner: your accountant deals with your past, while your financial planner deals with your future.

4. Most financial and insurance companies are very similar, and they offer similar products. One of the few things that distinguish between them is people. Spend time finding good advisors. It matters less what company they represent as long as they are good professionals that can save or make you money and protect your assets.

5. Never assume that your advisor knows what is best for you. You are the decision maker. Your advisor only provides recommendations. You should listen to their advice very attentively. If something does not make sense to you, you should either get a second professional opinion or dismiss the advice.

6. The easiest way to find out if your advisor has any conflict of interest is to ask about how they are compensated. The honest advisor will have no problem with this question.

7. A good advisor should ask many questions before proposing any products.

8. One dollar saved (after tax) is much more than one dollar earned (before tax). Every dollar matters.

9. When you spend your money, you spend time that you need to earn that money.

   a. The quality of your life depends on the income stream (cash flow) you have and not on the quantity of different assets you own. Your home where you live is not an asset because you spend money on it, and it does not generate any income.

   b. A reasonable amount of cash is a valuable resource (as long as inflation is low) when markets are falling. Do not listen to people who say otherwise.

   c. Losing money on an investment is a good experience, since you learn what not to do in the future. Everybody loses money at some point. Move on and do not be discouraged. Failure is the best teacher but only if you learn from it and move on.

10. You become wealthy not by getting astronomical rates of return on your investment (if you only invest $1, even a 300% rate of return will not make you rich), but by investing your own money on a periodic basis. The rate of return becomes an important factor only when you have a substantial amount of money to invest.

    a. The stock market and the economy are not the same thing. They can move in opposite directions.

    b. Try to diversify your sources of income; fully relying on CPP/OAS and RRIF payments is not the best option for retirement.

11. Plan to rely only on yourself and your own family. More and more baby boomers retire every year, and the government will not have enough money to subsidize everyone. What you earn prior to your retirement is what you will live on when you quit working.

12. There are no perfect investments. You can make or lose money on any investment. Investments themselves do not make or lose money, but buying or selling investments at the right or wrong time does. That is why it is important to buy investments when nobody wants them (and they are cheap). Even the Ponzi scheme (http://artemfinancial.ca/links/ponzi-scheme) can be a good investment if bought and sold at the right time. Unfortunately, if you buy a particular investment when it should be sold, it might take years before the price of the investment appreciates just to break even. Since it is difficult to know what will go up or down in price – diversify your investment and invest in different asset classes (i.e. do not invest all your money in your house assuming you can sell it when you retire).

13. Be ready for unpredictable financial events. Unpredictable events are rarely good. They always happen when you do not need them, and if you do not have extra money or insurance, your life might be ruined. Get a line of credit and/or insurance before you need it and when it is easier for you to qualify.

14. Banks and the government love inflation. You should invest in assets that will appreciate in value over time. There are no risk-free investments. All investments have some kind of risk, but the most dangerous of all are investments that people consider risk-free (e.g. GIC, government bonds). There is room for them in your portfolio, but they should not be held for a very long period of time because the inflation rate will be higher than the rate of return of the "no-risk" investments. On top of that, you have to pay taxes on the interest you earn in non-registered accounts.

15. Learn to be careful and practice simple ways to prevent identity theft and fraud, as they can happen to anybody.

GLOSSARY

Age of majority

The age of majority is 18 years in Alberta, Manitoba, Ontario, Prince Edward Island, Quebec and Saskatchewan. The age of majority is 19 in British Columbia, New Brunswick, Newfoundland, Nova Scotia, Northwest Territories, Nunavut, and Yukon.

The age of majority is the age at which a person is considered responsible for their decisions and can be bound by legal contracts.

Annuity

In exchange for a single lump sum investment, an insurance company pays out regular payments that include interest and a return of your capital. Annuity payments can continue for a chosen period of time or for the lifetime(s) of one or two people (usually spouses).

Annuities often offer a higher income rate than many other guaranteed income investments.

A particular type of annuity, called prescribed annuities, offers preferential tax treatment if your investments are non-registered. Each payment you receive has the same amount of interest and capital. This ensures that the taxable income is always the same and provides some tax deferral.

Asset Allocation

Asset allocation is the process of assigning various types of assets (cash, bonds, equities, real estate, and commodities) to your investment portfolio, based on your risk tolerance and your goals. At different points in your life, the exact composition of your portfolio may differ, as your risk tolerance, your goals, and/ or the market conditions change.

If you invest only in one asset class or all your money is invested in the same region of the world, your investment returns will exclusively depend on their performance. By diversifying your portfolio with different asset classes, you reduce some of your risk, since gains in one area can offset losses in another.

Bounced cheque

Bounced cheques are dishonoured cheques that have been returned due to non-sufficient funds (NSF) on the account, or because the account the cheque was written from has been closed. Both the party who wrote the cheque and the party who received it are charged an NSF fee by banks. If you have a good relationship with your bank and/or have a good reason to explain why the cheque bounced, the bank may refund the fee.

CMHC

The Canada Mortgage and Housing Corporation (CMHC) provides mortgage loan insurance to lenders for home buyers with a down payment of, typically, 5–20%. This insurance protects the lender, not the buyer. CMHC insurance guarantees the bank or credit union that it will not lose money on this high ratio mortgage (i.e. mortgage with a down payment less than 20%).

Corporation

A corporation is a widely used form of business organization, where the company and its shareholders (i.e. owners) each have separate legal standing. Incorporation protects the owners of the company from being personally liable in case the company is sued (which is referred to as "limited liability").

Caveat

Caveat means "let him beware" in Latin. It is a warning that someone is claiming an interest in a piece of land (or real estate).

Credit vs. Deduction

Tax credits reduce the amount of tax you pay. Tax deductions reduce your taxable income. For example, if you earned $50,000, then $10,000 in tax deductions means that your taxable income has been decreased to $40,000. $10,000 in tax credits means that you will save $10,000 on taxes.

Tax credits can be non-refundable and refundable. If you owe $8,000 of taxes, a refundable tax credit of $10,000 means that you will not pay any taxes and $2,000 will be refunded; a non-refundable tax credit of $10,000 means that you will still not pay any taxes, but you will receive no refund.

Deductibles

- A deductible is the amount of expenses that you must pay before your insurance company pays the coverage.

- A collision deductible is what you pay for getting your car fixed after an accident involving collision with another car or object.

- A comprehensive deductible is what you pay for getting your car fixed in case of a damage due to fire, theft, broken glass, or hitting an animal.

Deferred Profit Sharing Plan (DPSP)

A DPSP is linked to business profitability. The employer's contributions are made periodically, while employees do not contribute to the plan. Since there is no minimum requirement, there might be no contributions at all if there is no (or little) profit. However, CRA has set maximum contribution limits for the plan. A DPSP is only available as a group plan.

Defined Benefit Pension Plan (DB)

A plan where the employee receives a pension based on years of service and earnings. In a contributory plan, both the employee and the employer make contributions, while in a non-contributory plan, only the company is required to contribute to the plan.

Defined Contribution (DC) or Money Purchase Pension Plan

A plan where your pension is acquired via your company, based on your and your company's contributions, plus interest. The income you receive at retirement under a DC is not known in advance. It's based on the assets within your plan at the time you retire. You or your advisor decide which investments your contributions are invested in.

Discharge

A legal document stating that a loan has been fully repaid and releasing the borrower from any obligations.

Discount Broker

A business that offers fewer services and less support and therefore charges lower fees than a full-service broker. A discount broker assists clients with buying or selling securities, such as stocks and bonds.

Dividends

Taxable payments given to shareholders out of the company's earnings. Dividends can be in the form of cash, stock (stock dividend), or other property; however, companies are not required to pay them. In Canada, if you are both the owner AND an employee of your company, you might prefer to receive dividends rather than salary, tax-wise.

Exchange-Traded Fund (ETF)

A security that tracks an index, a commodity, or a basket of assets like an index fund, but trades like a stock on a stock exchange. ETF prices may fluctuate significantly throughout the day as they are bought and sold.

Exchange-Traded Notes (ETN)

Investments that are issued by financial institutions as senior debt notes.

ETF vs. ETN

Exchange-traded notes (ETNs) and exchange-traded funds (ETFs) are similar in many respects: both trade on stock exchanges and both are tied to an underlying index.

However, they differ in the risk of default. ETNs are unsecured debt; money is loaned in exchange for a promise of a return tied to an index. ETFs are pools of stocks (or other securities) in trust with a custodian. So if something happens to the issuing bank, the default risk for ETNs is much higher.

The second risk is related to liquidity. Since there are more ETFs than ETNs, buying and selling of ETNs may be more challenging, due to the lack of trading volume.

Estate

An estate is everything a deceased person owned (investments, cash, and personal items) minus all liabilities (debt and bills). If there is an estate, then liabilities and taxes of the deceased person have to be paid first before the beneficiaries can receive their assets. There are many legal ways of not including (some of) the deceased person's assets in the estate and transferring them to the beneficiaries directly.

Insurance Rider

An insurance rider provides the buyer with additional insurance or a modification to the standard policy. For example, the return of premium rider guarantees return of all paid premiums if the insured event does not take place within the insured period of time.

Land Titles Act

An act regulating registration of title for privately owned lands, under which the government has custody of the original documents and titles. The government is also accountable for the validity and security of the registered land title information.

Life Income Fund (LIF)

An investment where the holder receives taxable retirement income, based on chosen annuity factors. It is subject to the minimum amount (as per the Income Tax Act) and to the maximum amount (as per provincial Pension Benefits Acts).

Locked-in Retirement Account (LIRA)

An investment where your money is locked in the fund until you retire but continues to grow by accumulating interest. LIRAs and Registered Retirement Savings Plans (RRSPs) can have the same investments. LIRAs are governed by the provincial act.

Locked-in Retirement Income Fund (LRIF)

A RRIF investment that pays an adjustable amount of retirement income to the LRIF holder which is based on the investment income earned by the LRIF for the previous year.

Notice of Assessment (NOA)

A yearly statement issued by Canada Revenue Agency to taxpayers once the tax returns have been filed. This statement specifies the exact income, tax refunds, tax credits, and income tax that has been paid, as well as the amount that can be contributed to an RRSP.

Options

A binding contract that allows the buyer to buy or sell a particular asset at a specific price by a specified date. Similar to stocks and bonds, options are securities. Options can be of two types: calls and puts.

Prime Interest Rate

A guideline interest rate at which banks lend to high credibility customers. Banks and lenders in Canada follow the prime rate to remain competitive, but they may add or deduct their own spread to it. For example, when the prime lending rate is high, many lenders in Canada offer variable rates at prime minus 0.5–1%. When the prime rate is low, lenders may offer variable rates at prime plus 1%.

Premium

The premium is the amount paid by the policy holder and/or their plan sponsor (e.g. employer or union) for a fixed period of time to the insurance company for insurance coverage. Premiums depend on the buyer's age, health condition, duration of the insurance, sum assured, and type of policy.

Registered Retirement Income Fund (RRIF)

RRIF is a registered program, where you transfer investments from your RRSP. You have to withdraw at least the minimum (taxable) payment each year. The investment rules that apply to RRIFs are the same as those for RRSPs.

Superficial Loss

A capital loss which cannot be claimed since the sold property was re-acquired within 30 days after the disposition. Please visit http://artemfinancial.ca/links/superficial-loss to read more about superficial loss.

Tax Brackets

In Canada, we operate under a marginal tax rate system, which means that the more money we make, the more tax we pay. Marginal tax is the amount of tax paid on an additional dollar of income. For the marginal tax rates for 2013, see page 98 in "Managing your personal taxes" available at http://artemfinancial.ca/links/managing-taxes. To provide a concrete example drawing on this guide, if you reside in Alberta and your taxable income is $50,000, your marginal tax rate is 32%, but if your income is $90,000, your marginal tax rate is 36%. This is different than a flat tax rate where you pay the same rate of tax no matter what your income level is.

Underwriting

Evaluation of all the applicant's information, including but not limited to their credit history, employment, and net worth, to determine whether a credit application may be approved.

Article: Beware the pitfalls of collateral mortgages

By Mark Weisleder (Mark Weisleder is a lawyer, author, and speaker to the real estate industry. Email Mark at mark@markweisleder.com.) This essay has been reprinted with permission of the author.

When you apply for a mortgage, you usually just ask about the term, amount, interest rate and monthly payment. Not many people understand the difference between a conventional mortgage and a collateral mortgage. Yet many banks are now asking borrowers to sign collateral mortgages — and it could result in them being tied to this bank, for life.

With a normal conventional mortgage you bargain for a set amount, rate and amortization. Say the property is worth $250,000 — if you bargain for a $200,000 loan, at 3.5% for a five-year term with 25-year amortization, you will have payments of $998.54 per month.

A conventional mortgage is registered against the property for $200,000. If all the payments are made on time, the mortgage is renewed on the same terms every five years and no prepayments are made, the balance is zero after 25 years.

Should another lender decide to lend you money as a second mortgage, there is nothing stopping them from doing so, subject to their own guidelines. Under normal circumstances the principal balance on a conventional mortgage goes only one way, down. In addition, banks will accept "transfers" of conventional mortgages from other banks, at little or no cost to the consumer.

A collateral mortgage has as its primary security a promissory note or loan agreement and as "backup," a collateral security, being a mortgage against your property. The difference is that, in most cases, the mortgage will be for 125% of the value of the property. In the example, the mortgage registered will be for $312,500. But you will only receive $200,000. The loan agreement will indicate the actual amount of the loan, interest rate and monthly payments.

The collateral mortgage may indicate an interest rate of prime plus 5–10%. This will permit you to go back to this same bank and borrow more money from time to time, without having to register new security. The lender will offer you a closing service, to register the mortgage against your property, at fees that will be cheaper than what a lawyer would charge you. Sounds good so far, doesn't it?

However, this collateral loan agreement has different consequences, which are usually not explained to the borrower.

- Most banks will not accept "transfers" of collateral mortgages from other banks, so the consumer is forced to pay discharge fees to get out of one mortgage and additional fees to register a new mortgage if they move to a new lender. Thus the bank is able to tie you to them for all your lending needs indefinitely because it will cost you too much to move.

- Lenders may be able to use the collateral mortgage to offset any other unpaid debts you have. Offset is a right under Canadian law that says a lender may be able to seize equity you have in your home, over and above the mortgage balance, to pay, for example, a credit-card balance, a car loan, or any loan you may have co-signed that is in default with the same lender. In essence any loans you may have with that lender may be secured by the collateral mortgage. Nobody goes into a mortgage thinking about default, but "stuff" happens in people's lives and 25 years is a long time.

- Let's say your house value is $200,000. A collateral first mortgage registered on the property is $250,000. The amount owing on the mortgage is $150,000. If you were to need an additional $20,000, but the lender declines to lend it for any reason, then practically speaking you won't be able to approach any other lender. They will not go behind a $250,000 mortgage. Your only way out would be to pay any prepayment penalty to get out of the first mortgage and pay any additional costs to get a new mortgage.

- Let's say your mortgage is in good standing but you default under a credit line with the same bank. The bank could in most cases still start default proceedings under your mortgage, meaning you could lose the house.

- Some lenders are offering collateral mortgages in a "negative option billing" manner. Unless you are informed enough to say you want a conventional mortgage, you will be asked to sign documents for a collateral mortgage.

Please use this page for your notes.

Made in the USA
Charleston, SC
11 October 2015